8/6/14

Dear Sheila,

I trust your sciatica is sufficiently gone so you can come to the Arthritis Foundation next Tuesday. Surprise!

I also hope you like the book — especially the 10 tips to longevity.

Keep Young!

Ep. E.

My Century

To the adorable, darling, love of my life, Jean

My Century

EPHRAIM P. ENGLEMAN, M.D.

AS TOLD TO MATTHEW KRIEGER

CONTENTS

Section 1: Getting Started

1. Musical heart murmur   11
2. Early years   13
3. Rigid posture   16
4. Santa Cruz   18
5. Genius study   21
6. My mother, Tillie   23
7. My father, Morris   26
8. My marvelous showbiz career   33
9. Stanford years   38
10. Columbia: Anything goes   42
11. Jean: Dancin' to Anson   47
12. Finding my place   52

Section 2: Going Strong

13. The battle of Palm Springs   70
14. Home   76
15. Revolution in rheumatology   78
16. Goodbyes   80
17. The transformation of UCSF   84
18. Fiddles   86
19. Rosalind Russell and the National Commission   93
20. A very long way   101
21. The Family   105
22. The Other Family   110
23. Goodies   112
24. Ten tips on longevity   116

Family Tree, Ancestors   126
Family Tree, Descendants   128
Notes   130
Acknowledgments and photo credits   143

"A Happy New Year Sept. 13–14, 1920 from
Mr. & Mrs. Maurice Engleman, and their son Ephraim"

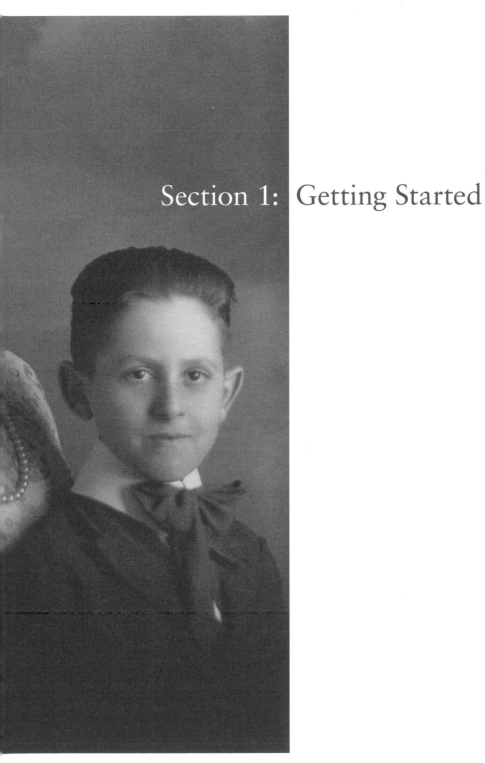

Section 1: Getting Started

1. Musical heart murmur

The turning point of my life came one December morning 72 years ago — I was 30 — when my musical talent saved me a second time from failure in medicine. After that morning, I knew what I was going to do with my life.

I had graduated in the bottom third of my medical school class at Columbia, and I knew it was a long shot when I applied for a rheumatology research fellowship with Dr. Walter Bauer at Massachusetts General Hospital. He was one of Harvard's most prominent physicians, and competition was fierce to work with him. At that time, 1940, rheumatology as a distinct field of American medicine had existed for only 12 years, and there were fewer than 20 trained rheumatologists in the country. Arthritis patients were cared for with the crude therapies of the time: huge doses of aspirin, gold salts, physical therapy, and inpatient bed rest, usually for weeks, sometimes for months. Wheelchairs and gurneys were very common.

During my interview with Dr. Bauer at Mass General, someone interrupted us to say it was time for ward rounds. Dr. Bauer asked me, "Would you like to join us?"

The ward for rheumatic disease patients was impressive — about 40 beds in one enormous open room and, I believe, the only dedicated rheumatology ward at the time. A group of us — fellows and junior physicians like me — trailed after Dr. Bauer, observing his warm interactions with each patient. He summarized for us the condition, treatment, and prognosis, and we could ask him questions or make comments.

We came to a woman in her sixties who had been brought into the hospital on a gurney. In addition to her arthritis, she had a musical heart murmur, a rare occurrence when the vibrations of a faulty heart valve sound a musical note that can be heard through a stethoscope. Walter asked for a phonocardiogram, a device to determine the note's rate of vibration. I listened through the stethoscope. Not being shy, I said I didn't need the machine, that it was around 500 vibrations. I had perfect pitch. I knew that A, the note the concertmaster plays to tune the orchestra's instruments, has 440 vibrations per second and that the murmur's note was a little sharper than A. I hit the nail on the head.

Dr. Bauer gave me an astonished look. "Forget the interview," he said. "You've got the job."

That is how I became a rheumatologist.

2. Early years

I was a spoiled child, and an only child until I was 16.

My mother's name was Tillie; her maiden name, Rosenberg. She was born in Manhattan in 1888, the fourth of seven children of Yiddish-speaking Polish immigrants who met in New York in the mid- or late 1870s and married there in 1880. Her family moved to San Francisco before she was two years old.

In 1895 my father, Morris Engleman, age ten, along with his eight-year-old sister, Bessie, left a Polish shtetl and sailed across the Atlantic in steerage to New York. Eventually, my widowed grandfather, Hirsh, arranged for them to travel by train to San Francisco, where he had settled.

Tillie and Morris met in San Francisco after my father befriended her brother, Harry. Harry owned a haberdashery, and that's where my father was working when my parents married in 1906 — she was 18, he was 21 — a few months after the great San Francisco earthquake and fire.

In the earthquake, the places where each lived were badly damaged. They took refuge in the open spaces of Golden Gate Park, west of the flames, in a makeshift tent city. Her tent was across from his. My mother often told the story — to great dramatic effect — that on their first morning in the park, my father would have been shot for turning on a water tap without permission if she had not thrown herself between him and the strict rule-enforcing soldier.

Sometime before my birth, my parents moved to San Jose, where they lived with my mother's parents, George and Bessie Rosenberg.

I was born in the middle of the night on March 24, 1911, at my parents' first San Jose home, on Park Avenue. As far as I know, it was an uncomplicated birth, assisted by a midwife.

When I was an infant, we moved to a house on the first block of South 9th Street, where we lived until I was seven or eight, when we moved to the house where I grew up: 78 South 13th Street, close to what is now San Jose State University. It's still standing. It is a small, one-story house in a nice part of San Jose.

All the rooms in our house were small: the kitchen, dining room, two bedrooms, and living room, where we had a small baby grand piano. My mother played piano a little, but it was purchased for me to play for pure pleasure. I never took piano lessons. I just picked it up.

Though there were two bedrooms, for reasons I was never told, I slept on the outdoor porch at the back of the house beyond the kitchen. It had no windows, just screens along the entire upper half of its three walls. Often I would just lie there on my bed and look out the window at the sky. In hot weather, my parents sometimes slept nearby in a double bed.

My maternal grandparents' home was on North 9th Street, within walking distance, but we always drove. Every year we went there for Passover seder. My grandfather always hid the matzo under the tablecloth near me, and I always knew where it was. When Elijah the prophet visited and sipped wine, my grandfather would wiggle the table to shake the wine a little. All of this was marvelous to me.

The school where I attended kindergarten and grade school was four blocks from home, yet my mother usually drove me both ways. As much as possible, she prevented me from walking anywhere. I rarely played outside; I might injure my hands. Consequently, I did not have many friends as a boy, although I was always an extrovert who loved to socialize and talk a lot.

3. Rigid posture

My earliest memory is learning to read music sitting on the potty.
My mother handed me sheets of music while I sat there. I could
read music before I could read words. She was ambitious for me to
become a fine violinist.

I practiced about an hour every day and had weekly lessons with
Niccolo DeLorenzo, a local teacher, in the music room he rented in
a San Jose home. My mother accompanied me to every lesson and
sat there quietly for the duration. Mr. DeLorenzo, pleased with my
playing, arranged for me to perform at a students' recital when I
was seven. While performing, a string broke, but I kept playing.
It was a sensation, written up in the *San Jose Mercury News*. I was
hailed as a prodigy.

The following year, through Mr. DeLorenzo's intervention —
I think my mother may have "encouraged" him a bit — the San
Francisco Symphony concertmaster, Louis Persinger, agreed to
hear me play. He didn't hear a prodigy, however, for good reason.
I see now that I studied violin to please my mother. I did not
discover a genuine enthusiasm for music until eight years later,
when I played jazz piano to entertain my friends.

San Jose, where we lived, was a backwater then, with a population
of fewer then 40,000. But the music scene in San Francisco was
booming, having come back to life after the 1906 earthquake and

fire destroyed all eight downtown theaters and the Opera House. The city was once again an important stop for illustrious performers from all over the world. This was before radio. Victrolas were still fairly primitive and, like most families, we didn't own one. The only way to hear music was to hear it live.

As a special treat, about once a year my parents took me to a concert in San Francisco. The most thrilling was when, at the age of eight, I heard Jascha Heifetz — heralded on the program cover as "The World's Greatest Violinist" — at a Sunday afternoon recital at the Columbia Theatre, what's now the American Conservatory Theater. Heifetz was only 19 then, but he had been performing in public for nine years.

That day he played a Paganini caprice. In the 90-plus years of hearing great violinists since then, I have never heard a more triumphant performance. He had it all in spades: technique, intonation, and phrasing. I was astonished that such magnificent music was being created by a man with such rigid posture. Violinists today move all over the place. Not Heifetz. Except for his arms, he never moved. Because of that, quite a few people said he was a cold player. If you really listened, you could not possibly think his playing was cold. He was a great artist.

4. Santa Cruz

From the time I was six until I finished high school, we would spend at least six weeks in Santa Cruz every summer. It was just my mother and I during the week. My father would come on weekends. We almost always stayed in the same simple, two-story hotel right across the street from the beach. A number of relatives on my mother's side of the family would join us for a week or two. They always stayed elsewhere. I don't know why.

I loved Santa Cruz. I loved getting there, too. We would take one train from San Jose to Los Gatos, nothing but fruit orchards mile after mile. Then we'd take another train to Santa Cruz along a spectacular mountain forest route.

Most days my mother and I would spend about four hours on the beach, sitting on blankets under an umbrella, talking. We would go into the ocean, but not beyond the breakers because I could not swim. Usually we would have lunch on the boardwalk and in the evening ride the streetcar into town for dinner. Some days we would go to the Plunge, a huge indoor saltwater swimming pool right off the boardwalk. My mother decided that I needed to learn to swim. Instead of paying for lessons, she watched the swimming teacher with his students and copied his methods as best she could.

I was never a very good swimmer.

Ephraim at 2 or 3.

Ephraim (Eph) at 13.

5. Genius study

One of my teachers must have told Lewis Terman about me because when I was five, I was enrolled in what turned out to be the pilot study for a Stanford University investigation that got lots of press for decades: "The Genetic Study of Genius." Its purpose was to better understand intellectually gifted children, with whom Terman was obsessed.

Lewis Terman was one of Stanford's early stars, and he was the best-known psychologist in the country. He coined the term *intelligence quotient* (IQ) after he and his colleagues translated and introduced this country's first standardized intelligence test, originally formulated by French psychologists Alfred Binet and Théodore Simon. Terman called the test the Stanford-Binet Intelligence Scales. It has been revised four times since, but it's still widely in use.

When I enrolled, the project involved about a hundred children with IQs of 130 or higher. At its peak in 1928, there were more than 1,500 individuals participating.

The study was supposed to end in 1925, but Terman couldn't give up his "gifted children," which is what he called us even as adults. We called ourselves Termites. It is the first example in science of a prospective study—one where people are followed over many years to identify how factors in earlier life affect them decades later.

This format was a brilliant idea and perhaps Terman's greatest contribution to science. For about 85 years — that is, until maybe a decade ago — I got surveys in the mail every five or ten years. I filled out questionnaires that asked me whether I was satisfied with my marriage and my sex life, how much money I earned, what political party I belonged to, whether I was religious and, of course, about my physical and mental health.

Terman's research has been called into question, according to a 2000 *Stanford Magazine* article, because of its homogeneity and other design flaws. But from what I understand, any shortcomings are far outweighed by the pioneering nature of his studies and his findings, some of which opened up new lines of research.

The *Stanford Magazine* article also said that quite a few Termites felt that the study had changed their lives. But it never meant much to me, perhaps because I was only five when it began. My parents must have been proud, but I don't remember them ever saying anything about it. I took the test, answered the questions, and completed the forms. And that was about it.

The massive quantities of information Terman collected about us for most of the twentieth century has turned out to be one of the most valuable collections of data for today's social science investigators, who are mining it to answer questions — about longevity, for example — that never crossed Terman's mind.

6. My mother, Tillie

My mother was in charge of everything in our family, including my father. To describe her as "authoritarian" is perhaps a bit too harsh, but it's close. She was a tough cookie who did not let her guard down, and she made her expectations very clear. I didn't dare disregard her wishes. I never misbehaved.

She was enormously ambitious for both her boys — me and my brother Maurice, who was born when I was 16. She was determined to make us both world-class violinists. I have no idea why she was so fixated on this idea. She never had much exposure to classical music. And while she tinkered a little on the piano, she was not a musician.

My father did not earn much money, or at least that's the impression I had as a boy. My mother certainly lived as if that were true. She grew up in poverty, one of nine people in the household. Her father started out as a cigarette peddler on the Lower East Side, one of hundreds of thousands of immigrant Jews struggling to survive. All her life, cost was the foremost consideration in food shopping. During the Depression, this was a necessity, but she didn't have to shop this way after my father recovered financially. She would still walk ten blocks to save a couple of pennies on day-old bread.

I sat down to her meals with dread. It's not so much that she ruined food. It just never tasted good. She had learned her way around the kitchen from her mother Bessie, who I'm pretty sure was the worst cook on the planet at the time. To this day, my stomach turns when I think of her beef liver — not liver and onions, mind you, just liver. It has crossed my mind that she might have sold the recipe to the Florsheim Shoe Company. She also cooked tongue, which was very inexpensive. I refused to eat that, as well as lung, which my father liked. We never ate pork, but we did not keep kosher. Also, we never had alcohol in the house, not even wine. The only time we had wine was at Passover seder, which was at my grandparents' home.

Like most Jewish married women, my mother had a *knipple*, a stash she squirrelled away from the household money, five cents here, a dollar there.

My brother tells the story that when he was five, my father came home for lunch, as he did every day, extremely upset, and he told my mother that if he didn't come up with $5,000 right away, they were going to lose the house and the store. It was during the Depression. My mother said, "Why don't you call Cousin Isidor and ask him for the money?" referring to Isidor Marcus, a successful furrier in town and her cousin. He left the house immediately to visit Cousin Isidor. The moment my father was out the door, my mother called her cousin and said, "Isidor, Maurice will be at your store in a very short time. He's going to ask for a $5,000 loan. Give it to him. I'll reimburse you. And charge him six percent."

When my father died in 1953, my brother and my mother were alone together in the back of the mortuary limousine riding from the funeral parlor to the cemetery when she recounted the incident, confirming his memory of it and revealing that my father had repaid Isidor the loan, never knowing its true source, nor that his wife got all the interest.

My mother was nearly inseparable from her sister, my Aunt Rose, ten years younger, the baby of the family, a very sweet woman who also lived in San Jose. My mother was also extremely close to her parents, George and Bessie Rosenberg. They lived in San Jose until I was 16 or 17, when they moved back to San Francisco for the rest of their lives. When George and Bessie were old and ill, my mother and Rose went to see them often, as much as twice a week. In those days, it was a long trip from San Jose to San Francisco. They were devoted daughters and they must have dearly loved my grandparents.

Unlike my father, my mother was not affectionate. Despite her tough exterior, I never doubted her love for me. All my life, she beamed with pride at my achievements: an A student, gifted violinist, orchestra member, music director, medical student and, of course, doctor. Surprisingly, when she gave up her dream for me to be a concert violinist, she did so very easily. It makes me wonder if "my son, the doctor" was her true ambition for me all along.

7. My father, Morris

My father told us he came from a Polish shtetl called Ulick — or some phonetic variation of that word — but he never wrote it down. I've searched extensively to find it and cannot, even in histories of shtetls. It has disappeared off the maps. So I don't know in what part of Poland, which was controlled by Russia then, my father and his people lived.

His father, Hirsh Engleman, left his wife and two children behind in Ulick in 1893, when he was 28, and emigrated via Germany to the United States, settling in San Francisco for unknown reasons. At that time, my father was eight years old and his sister Bessie was six. The plan was that his family would join him when Hirsh could send money for their passage.

But my grandmother died, leaving my father and Bessie in the care of relatives or neighbors. Communal spirit was the centerpiece of shtetl life, and giving to the needy was a sacred duty. Temporarily orphaned, my father and aunt were probably in good hands. In 1895, two years after he left for America, Hirsh sent enough money for Morris and Bessie to cross the Atlantic on a steamship in steerage, the cheapest passage. Morris was ten and Bessie was eight. They traveled without adult supervision.

According to accounts by countless Europeans who made similar passages, my father and aunt would have been packed with hundreds of other immigrants into the mostly dark cargo hold and largely confined there for nine days. During the crossing, they were subjected to the stench of decomposing food, human waste, and vomit—toilets were few and primitive. They bunked together on a straw mattress in full view of others, keeping warm with blankets they brought from home. Fleas and lice thrived in this environment, as did cholera, smallpox, yellow fever, and other communicable diseases. Mortality rates were high.

Adults amused themselves by singing, dancing, gambling, playing cards, and talking—anything to counter the stupefying boredom of long days and nights at sea. For unsupervised children, there was only danger.

My father never spoke of the journey, but he did often say that there was no one to greet them when they arrived in New York. They were on their own in a new country with no knowledge of its language, culture, or currency and with only a few dollars.

Because they spoke Yiddish, and there was a huge population of other Jewish immigrants there, they must have fit fairly quickly into what was called the Jewish Lower East Side. They found a hayloft to live in, above the horses in a fire station, and ate pumpernickel bread and bananas. He got a menial job and was very proud of the large silver coin he earned every week: a 50-cent piece.

Both my brother and I clearly remember our father telling us repeatedly he became a child actor in the Yiddish Art Theater. But it turns out this is impossible because this celebrated company wasn't founded until 1918, when my father was 33 years old and had been in the Bay Area for about 20 years. He probably did some acting in some Yiddish theater productions, of which there were dozens, in the Lower East Side when he lived there.

I don't know how long it was before my grandfather, Hirsh, sent money from San Francisco for Morris and Bessie to take the train to San Francisco and join him.

Eventually my father — whose real name was Maurice and was known to many people as Moishe — got the job in Harry Rosenberg's shop in San Francisco. After my parents married and relocated to San Jose, he worked in his father-in-law's — George Rosenberg's — haberdashery. Later he owned his own shop. It was on Market at Post Street in San Jose, diagonally across the street from George's shop. I spent a lot of time in both places.

The sign outside my father's store read California Loan Office, a rather prestigious sounding name for a small business that was part pawnshop, part haberdashery. The display windows on either side were filled with inexpensive shirts, ties, pants, socks, handkerchiefs, and hats. Packaged and loose underwear lay out on tables. The front door was always open, and inside there was more of the same, all on tables standing on worn wooden floors. There were no mannequins or display cases. The store wasn't that fancy. There were no suits or jackets or anything else that required fitting.

Eph with his mother, Tillie, on vacation in Santa Cruz, 1925.

Eph with his father, Morris, 1925.

The loan office was in the back, a little room with bars on a window without glass where I often saw my father bent over a piece of jewelry with his hand-held loupe pressed to his right eye. Upstairs, in the back of the small private mezzanine, there was a cot, where he took a nap every day.

My father was emotionally and culturally Jewish, but he was not religious. Despite this, he led the fundraising drive to rebuild our synagogue, Bichur-Cholin Temple, San Jose's only synagogue, when it burned down, and he was the first president of the new shul, renamed Temple Emanu-El, a position he held for about ten years. In 2012 I had the privilege of speaking at a ceremony at the temple when a plaque honoring my father was dedicated.

I didn't realize it when I was young, of course, but my father was an exceptional person. He was a very giving human being: warm, kind, and generous to everyone he crossed paths with. I'm sure many people were amused by him, by his accent, by his mangling of the English language. But he did it all with such charm and with such a wonderful, gracious sense of humor. He was just a lovely guy.

My grandfather Hirsh came to visit us only two or three times over the years. He was a tailor who lived in San Francisco, then moved to Berkeley, where he had his own shop. He was an odd duck, with an obsession with cleanliness. He would wash his hands at least once an hour and always immediately after shaking hands with anyone. I remember watching in disbelief as he cleaned the Venetian blinds at our house with a towel because he couldn't stand any dust.

Life didn't turn out well for Aunt Bessie, my father's sister. She married a man named Aaron Cohn, who was reputedly handsome, charming, and rich, and they lived in Portland, Oregon. Mr. Cohn had an affair with their housekeeper and made no effort to keep it secret from Aunt Bessie. She declined steeply into what in those days was called melancholia and was institutionalized at the Agnew State Hospital for the mentally ill, near San Jose, for the rest of her life. She visited us two or three times, but she never said a word. After her death, her husband married the housekeeper.

8. My marvelous showbiz career

My life became a lot more fun in high school. I became popular. During lunch hour, I played jazz on the piano in the school auditorium, and the other kids gathered around to listen. I may be the only student ever to attend San Jose High School who earned a varsity letter for sports who did not play on a team and who was, in fact, the most unathletic guy you could imagine. Coach Lou Vogt, the basketball coach, a really nice guy, overheard me playing. He thought the jazz would have an invigorating effect on the players and improve their game, so he asked me to play an hour or more during practice. At the end of the year I proudly marched across the stage with the athletes to pick up the red cloth patch with the 8-inch letters "SJ" from Coach Vogt.

I joined the drama club — my biggest part was Shylock — and found out I loved being on stage.

Two things did not change. First, I continued to excel academically. Second, my mother drove me to and from school. It was still only four blocks from home.

The greatest adventure of my early life began shortly after I graduated from high school in 1927, when San Jose got its first plush movie palace. The 1,800-plus-seat Fox California Theater was the only place in town with both first-run silent movies and live entertainment. It was also the first theater in San Jose to have an orchestra. The building today is the California Theatre, home to Opera San Jose and Symphony Silicon Valley.

When it opened, theater management needed two violinists, one of whom had to come from a local union, but the local union didn't have any violinists. Somehow they heard about me. After much discussion, my parents and I agreed I'd take the job. I joined the union and, at 16, I was making $75 per week — very good pay in those days — playing full-time while also attending college part-time at San Jose State Teachers College, which is now San Jose State University.

Every movie came with its own musical score and we had, at most, two hours to rehearse the music before the first screening. We also had a run-through for the live entertainers — each act gave us its music. During the movie we played in the orchestra pit, and for the live show we moved on the proscenium stage to seats set up behind the performers.

The live entertainment usually lasted about 40 minutes and consisted of three or four unrelated acts — acrobats, opera singers, banjo players, ballet dancers, magicians, animal acts, comedians, jugglers, just about anything. But there were almost always chorus girls. Of course, this was family entertainment fare, so the girls' costumes and kicks were on the wholesome side. My mother, father, and my little brother Maurice would come at least one evening a week and usually sit close to where I was playing.

Eph (right) and vaudeville skit partner, Jay Brower, at the Fox California
Theatre, San Jose, about 1929.

To my pal Les -
Lots of good luck
and success —
don't forget our good
times I
Yours for a ten
"Eph" '3

Eph, music director and showman, Fox California Theatre, about 1931.

After about a year and a half, I started doing skits onstage with the music director, Jay Brower. I was six-foot-two and he was short. We thought this height difference would make us a team, and it did. We'd tell jokes and do gags—I don't remember any of them—and I learned how to tap dance a little. I also developed a talent for humor on stage and a sense of timing, which has stayed with me all my life.

I was a big shot. There was a lot of publicity in San Jose for the theater—newspaper advertisements and billboards—and my name was prominent. So when I went to school at the teacher's college, everyone knew me. This was a great time for me, and I met so many cute girls. I replaced Jay about 1931 as the music director and master of ceremonies, which meant I introduced the various acts to the audience. My salary was doubled to $150 per week, and I bought myself a used Ford. I was with the orchestra nearly five years and I loved every minute of it.

Then came the talkies. When *The Jazz Singer,* starring Al Jolson, opened down the street, we were no longer the best entertainment in town. Very quickly it became obvious that my musical career was finished. This turned out to be a great blessing. My parents and I talked about my future, and all of us agreed that I would transfer from San Jose State Teacher's College to Stanford University, and then go to medical school. I was happy with this decision.

9. Stanford years

In September 1931, when I was 20, I entered Stanford as a junior. Tuition was $300 per year, which I was able to pay from savings from my years with the orchestra.

Going to Stanford was a big change and a welcome one. For one thing, I lived on campus — my first experience living away from home, and I loved that. I lived in Sequoia Hall, a three-story men's dorm on Serra Street that housed about 80 guys. It was originally a women's dorm and had been renovated when converted to a men's dorm after a larger women's dorm was built. It was pretty run down by the time I got there.

Another thing: I wasn't working, so I could devote all my attention to my pre-med studies.

That was the idea, anyway. In reality, the transition from vaudeville and chorus girls to serious academia was not an easy one. I still had show business in my blood. I spent a lot of my time working on productions for Stanford's Ram's Head Dramatic Society, the Junior Opera, and the Masque Ball — sometimes behind the scenes, sometimes on stage.

I pretty much put on the 1932 Stanford Gaieties, an annual student show performed the week before the Big Game with Cal, begun in 1911 and continuing to this day. In my time the Gaieties was a wacky, wickedly funny piece of musical theater featuring unrelated topical skits crammed with in-jokes, spoofs, and gags. The traditional audition motto was, "Enthusiasm, not talent." The fact that I had both talent and enthusiasm was most welcome. I was the master of ceremonies and also accompanied myself on piano singing a tune I wrote just for the show called, "Nobody Knows What Heaven Is Like Until You've Kissed a Redheaded Girl." "The cast is top-notch," wrote a reviewer in *The Quad,* Stanford's yearbook, "with Eph Engleman heading up the comedy; Eph doesn't need a script to draw the laughs."

I was the master of ceremonies at the next year's Masque Ball as well and got soundly panned for it in *The Quad.* "Masque Ball Is Fizzle," went the headline. "Looked forward to by few, enjoyed by less, and remembered by none…" The reviewer was right about the last part, at least. I don't remember any of the skits. "An Engleman orgy," is what the yearbook reviewer called it. Maybe it was. It was that much fun.

Not surprisingly, my grades were not very good and it was obvious I was going to have a hard time getting into medical school.

Somehow I made the acquaintance of Lucie Stern, the philanthropic and very wealthy widow of Louis Stern, one of the four nephews who inherited most of the fortune accumulated by blue jeans manufacturer Levi Strauss when he died in 1902. I think whoever introduced us thought she'd like me because of my experience in show business and theater, which were among her great interests.

Mrs. Stern hosted dinner parties nearly every Sunday night for eight to ten male students at her home at 1990 Cowper Street in Palo Alto. In the Spanish Colonial Revival style, it had just been built by Birge Clark, whose prolific architectural output greatly influenced the look of the entire town then and now. It was elegant and comfortable, but not showy or ostentatious; a one-story, detached home with stucco walls and chimneys outside and in, and a low-pitched clay tile shed roof. It's still standing. Mrs. Stern had an adjoining similar house at 1950 Cowper built for her invalid daughter, Ruth, at the same time.

I always felt at ease and welcome. Mrs. Stern, in her early sixties then, was a warm and gracious hostess. She was not particularly pretty. She dressed nicely and traditionally, without much jewelry or makeup. We hit it off, and after a while I realized I was the only student invited almost every week.

The dinners, prepared by her French chef, Eugene, were not the multi-course gourmet affairs you might expect. They were closer to a good home-cooked meal, which was in itself a new experience for me after 20 years at my mother's dining table. The ambiance at these parties was casual and relaxed. We'd sit at her big round table talking about anything and everything, from football games to movies to professors we liked and didn't like.

Mrs. Stern was called "the fairy godmother of Palo Alto" because of the dozen or so major civic projects she made possible by her philanthropy. One is the Palo Alto Community Theater, located in the community center that bears her name, which she paid for in

1933, the year I graduated. She also contributed a lot of money to Stanford — a dorm and a professorship are named for her.

How she did it, I don't know, but I am convinced Mrs. Stern pulled some strings to get me into Columbia Medical School. My grades were just not strong enough for me to be admitted to such a prestigious school. Stanford turned me down and I didn't bother applying to the University of California, San Francisco, because I didn't think I had much of a chance.

I introduced Mrs. Stern to a girl I was dating named Betty, and Mrs. Stern became quite attached to her. She was a gentile girl I met at San Jose State Teacher's College. My mother, of course, didn't like that I was going out with a gentile, and eventually I broke it off mainly for that reason, but I would have broken it off anyway.

When I married the love of my life, Jean Sinton, eight years later, we invited Mrs. Stern to the wedding. But she declined, saying she felt I had been disloyal to Betty. She never even met Jean, which is a shame because I think they would have liked each other. I lost touch with Mrs. Stern when I married Jean in 1941.

10. Columbia: Anything goes

The first time my musical talent saved me from failure in medicine was when I was a first-year student at the Columbia University College of Physicians & Surgeons in New York. Although I worked hard, I struggled mightily with the required basic science classes — anatomy, biochemistry, physiology, and others. In fact, I am convinced I would have been thrown out had it not been for the intervention of Dr. Hans Smetana, a highly respected pathology professor I got to know playing music.

Dr. Smetana and I played together frequently, and rather spontaneously, on Sundays in the lounge on the ground floor of my dorm, Bard Hall, which looked out on the Hudson River. He was a grand-nephew of Bedrich Smetana, the great Czech composer, whose work includes "The Moldau" and "The Bartered Bride." Usually it was only the two of us, me on the violin, him on the grand piano in one corner of the room. Mostly we played sonatas by Beethoven, Mozart, and others. Occasionally, other professors would join us, and we'd play chamber music. During these impromptu sessions, sometimes a handful of students would drift in and listen, sitting in easy chairs and on couches scattered throughout the room. When I played solo jazz piano in the lounge, which I did several weekday evenings each week, 15 or 20 fellow students would gather around, just like in high school.

I came up with the idea to put on a senior show, which I directed and performed in. We did skits and sang popular songs, changing the lyrics to lampoon faculty members. One parody I particularly remember was aimed at a neurosurgeon named Stookey, who wore a tab collar and necktie, a fashion introduced by Edward, Prince of Wales that we found ridiculous. Fashion was never in fashion at Columbia.

The highlight of every week was going to a Broadway musical. I'd jump on the subway a block away at 168th Street, and 15 minutes later be in line to buy a standing-room-only ticket for a buck — usually I'd sneak into an empty seat after the lights went down. I saw practically every new show for four years. This was heaven.

Without question, the greatest show I saw was George and Ira Gershwin's *Porgy & Bess*. But it ran for less than four months. It was mostly panned by critics and public alike. There had never been anything like it, and people didn't know what to make of it. Its score blended jazz, classical, and popular styles. It had an all-black cast, unheard of then. And it was a serious show in the depths of the Great Depression, when lighthearted, escapist musical comedies drew the crowds.

Cole Porter did the escapist stuff better than anyone, with his insider's perspective on high society and carefree living. It's no wonder he had more hit musicals in the 1930s than any other songwriter. I saw all his shows, and I loved them all. I still do. *Anything Goes* is one of my favorites.

Another favorite was the Rodgers and Hart musical *On Your Toes*. Not only was the music brilliant — "There's a Small Hotel" and "It's Got to Be Love" — but I was knocked out seeing George Balanchine's ballet *Slaughter on Tenth Avenue* integrated into a Broadway musical.

On the academic front, I did a bit better in year three, when we had our first direct patient contact during closely supervised hospital visits. I had much more interaction with patients during year four. I was surprisingly comfortable with it. In fact, I liked it a lot.

I was without doubt in the lower third of my graduating class. Maybe that's why I skipped the commencement ceremony, opting instead for a cheap, shared cabin on a ship to San Francisco via the Panama Canal. The highlight was a brief stop in Havana. I made a beeline to what I had been told were the best night clubs, and that's where I heard Cuban music for the first time.

I came back to the Bay Area to start an internship at Mt. Zion Hospital in San Francisco. Today it's part of UCSF. Then it was an independent Jewish hospital. The doctors were almost all Jewish, and so were many of the patients. In those days, Jewish doctors couldn't work at some San Francisco hospitals. Quotas were common. I know Columbia medical school had one when I was there. I was certainly aware of the anti-Semitism, but I don't think it disturbed me at all. My attitude was: everyone knows I'm Jewish, and I make no bones about it. As far as what they say when I'm not around — I don't know and I don't care.

My internship at Mt. Zion was not a prestige gig. It was widely considered to be a second-rate institution then, which is why I was able to get a job there and not at UCSF, where I wanted to be. I worked long hours, and I genuinely enjoyed the intimacy of the doctor-patient relationship. I discovered clinical medicine was my calling. As an intern, I did well enough to be told by Harold Rosenblum and John Sampson, associate chiefs of medicine, that I would be given a residency in medicine the next year, which delighted me.

But that decision was trumped by Dr. Leroy Briggs, the chief of medicine at both Mt. Zion Hospital and San Francisco County Hospital (San Francisco General now). He was their superior and he chose someone else for the job. I was crushed. If I've ever gone through a period of depression in my life, it was then. It felt like my career in medicine was a disaster. I can't think of another period in my life when I felt so terrible.

As it happened, Briggs, Rosenblum, and Sampson worked out a compromise and offered me a residency in pathology at Mt. Zion, even though I had no interest in pathology. This turned out to be another blessing. The head of pathology — his name was Rusk — was a rather old man, very highly respected throughout the community, not just at Mt. Zion. He was recognized as the leading — certainly one of the leading — pathologist in the city. So he was a very fine contact.

As a resident in pathology, I was part of a small team that did autopsies on almost every patient who died in the hospital. In fact, there was a rule that you had to do a certain number of autopsies. A clinical pathology conference (CPC) was held regularly, at which time interesting cases and their pathologic lines were presented. Not only Mt. Zion people attended. Doctors from other local hospitals came too, including Dr. Briggs.

For some reason, and I can't remember why, I became interested in cancer of the pancreas. So I did a retrospective study of ten years of data from autopsied patients who died of it at Mt. Zion and two other San Francisco hospitals. It was original research that today is not particularly important, but in those days was significant because it suggested that blood in the stool could be a sign for pancreatic cancer. I prepared a paper on this and presented it at one of the CPCs where Dr. Briggs was present. He was impressed by this paper—enough so that he recommended me for a medical residency at UCSF, and that's how I got into UC.

Just when things were looking up, they got better. Much better, in fact — and in a way that has made me very happy for the 75 years since. I met the woman of my dreams, my darling wife, Jean Sinton.

11. Jean: Dancin' to Anson

I was set up on a blind date. An acquaintance named Marjory Bissinger invited me to escort her cousin, Jean Sinton, to a charity event at the Fairmont Hotel. My first impression of Jean was that she was very pretty and bright, but also very young. She looked to be about 16, although she was 21. Jean is small: barely five feet tall, and she weighed 105 pounds when we met.

I picked her up at the home of her friend Joan Salz. Jean offered me a drink, and I said, "Thank you, but I don't drink." She offered me a cigarette, and I said, "Thank you, but I don't smoke." Months later she told me she assumed I was an athlete in training, which is funny because I'm one of the least athletic people I know.

Jean was a heck of a good dancer, and we had a marvelous evening. Anson Weeks and his 15-piece orchestra played. They were a local "hotel band" that made it pretty big nationally. "Dancin' to Anson" became popular everywhere after Weeks recorded a best-selling record with Bing Crosby and started broadcasting his "Lucky Strike Magic Carpet" radio program live, coast-to-coast, from the Mark Hopkins Hotel.

During the evening, Jean and I remembered that we had met once before, earlier that year at the Beresford Country Club — a Jewish golf club in San Mateo — where her father had been president. Today it's the Peninsula Golf and Country Club and non-sectarian.

I had been invited to a party there. Jean was dancing on stage in some kind of amateur show. We were introduced, and I thought she was very cute. The only words I remember saying to her that night were, "How do you do?"

We began dating. She did volunteer work at Mt. Zion, so we'd get together when I got off work. Often we'd go to a little upstairs hole-in-the-wall Chinese restaurant somewhere on Grant Avenue and afterward go dancing, either at the Fairmont Hotel or the St. Francis.

Jean lived with her parents "in the country" — that's how we referred to the woodsy Hillsborough of those days. It was about a 45-minute drive along El Camino, which we called "the highway," even though in Millbrae it passed a dairy farm with cows. Jean was very down-to-earth, and I was always perfectly comfortable with her. But I was a little uncomfortable in her home.

The Sinton house had eight bedrooms, a spectacular staircase, and an enormous living room with a huge travertine marble fireplace. It sat on two and a half acres. There was a barn for the pony that Jean had when she was younger. The Sintons had four full-time servants: a Danish cook, a French governess for the younger of Jean's two sisters, a German upstairs maid, and a houseboy who waited on table and cleaned. Jean was given her own car when she was 15, which she always drove cross-legged — something I've never seen, nor even heard of, any other woman do.

Jean's parents, Edgar Sinton and Marian Walter Sinton, were each born in San Francisco into wealthy, socially prominent German Jewish families that were closely connected. Jean was born in San Mateo in 1915, the first of three girls. When she was four, the family moved into the Hillsborough house they had built, and about that time the entire clan changed its surname from Sinsheimer to Sinton. It had been uncomfortable having such a German name during World War I, so they decided to play down their heritage.

Jean went to public grade school, then to the exclusive, non-sectarian, all-girl middle/high school Castilleja, whose motto at the time was "The five Cs: conscience, courtesy, character, courage and charity." Though she hated school, her parents persuaded her to go to Mills College, where she lived on campus. She quit after three years. She had had enough of all-girl environments.

I've been told Jean had many proposals, and I don't doubt it. She was extremely popular. Perhaps that's why her father was overprotective. Sometimes on a date she'd look in the rearview mirror and see her father in his car following. Long after we were married, Jean told me her father used to make up funny names and rhymes for her boyfriends. Mine was "Ephoo, ifoo, give me a piece of pie-foo." Her mother said if he didn't knock it off, Jean would never get married.

After we had been dating for two years, Jean's father summoned me to his Montgomery Street law office and asked how serious

I was about his daughter. He wasn't convinced, I found out later, that I could keep her in the style to which she was accustomed. I told him I was, indeed, serious about Jean. Not long afterward, I gave her a beautiful diamond ring—I got it from my father, who must have had it in his shop. I don't think she's ever taken it off.

I began the medical residency at UCSF in 1939. I did well, and Dr. William J. Kerr, Chairman of the UCSF Department of Medicine, recommended me for my third one-year residency—this one at the Joseph H. Pratt Diagnostic Hospital in Boston, part of Tufts University. And so, after a year at UCSF, I was off to Boston.

Jean and I didn't see each other for seven months. We kept in touch through frequent letters, since long-distance phone calls were outrageously expensive. We got engaged during my first trip back to the Bay Area in February 1941.

Because my schedule as a doctor in training at the Pratt was so inflexible, we decided to get married just a month after we became engaged. With so little time to plan, Jean and her mother decided it would be a "small" wedding, with about 150 guests, at the Sinton home. Jean's mother called the St. Francis Hotel and let them handle just about everything, including putting up a transparent tent on the terrace next to the house big enough to accommodate everyone at a sit-down dinner. It was a good thing, too, because it rained that day, March 2, 1941.

The marriage ceremony was in the living room, officiated by a rabbi from Temple Emanu-El. Jean's sister Ruth—the sister she was closer to — couldn't be her attendant because she was in the final months of pregnancy. Her younger sister, named Marian after their mother, was her maid of honor. My brother Maurice was my best man.

My parents met Jean's parents for the first time at the wedding. Looking back, I see that I was a little embarrassed by my father, with his thick Yiddish accent and poor grammar, talking with the Sintons. I was so wrong about him because he was such a remarkable man. But I was immature about such things — that's just how I thought then.

One of the things everyone remembers about the wedding is my mother crying the biggest tears ever shed by a human being. These were not tears of joy. My mother had a long list of reasons why I shouldn't get married: She said I was too young. (I was three weeks shy of 30.) She said I should wait until I was earning a good living. She said Jean "wasn't Jewish enough" because she didn't go to synagogue, even on the high holidays. She said the class difference between our family and the Sintons was too great. On our wedding day, she kept these thoughts to herself. But she could not hide her sorrow at losing her son. That was the real reason she didn't want me to get married. Through her sobs, my mother said to Jean, "You're getting an angel," to which Jean responded, "I know."

Within a couple of months, my wife and my mother were on great terms — in fact, they were corresponding every day — and their very friendly relationship continued until my mother died 20 years later.

12. Finding my place

The night Jean and I got married, we boarded a train for Boston and the Pratt, where I was doing my residency. Then, as now, it was quite unusual to have three one-year residencies at different hospitals, and the reason was not flattering. I just don't think I was capable enough to take the next step up, which would have been to be named a chief resident. And I didn't feel prepared to leave academia and go out and practice medicine. I was feeling adrift. I knew a residency was the path to specialization, but I had no idea what I wanted to do in medicine.

In Boston, we rented a little apartment, I don't remember where. Jean did volunteer work in a clinic at the Pratt, and she won my mother's heart by writing her a letter every day — something she continued doing for the next couple of years.

My residency at the Pratt was much like UCSF. I had a great deal of responsibility for treating adult medical patients — both inpatients and outpatients — under the supervision of very good attending physicians.

While I was there, my paper on cancer of the pancreas was published in the *Bulletin of the New England Medical Center —* my first publication.

Somehow I heard about the training fellowship in rheumatology at the Harvard-affiliated Massachusetts General Hospital. I didn't know much about arthritis and didn't have any particular interest in it. I knew the fellowship would be hard to get because Walter Bauer was an important guy at Harvard. I went to the interview pretty much thinking, "What do I have to lose?" and landed the job thanks to my perfect pitch.

Working with Dr. Bauer at Mass General, I spent my time treating arthritis patients. It's hard to imagine now, but in the early 1940s rheumatology clinics were packed with patients in wheelchairs and on crutches. Of course, it had been that way forever. If you had severe arthritis, it was a given that you had to live with a lot of pain and very limited mobility. Many patients were not only homebound, but permanently bedridden and almost completely dependent on others.

There was nothing we doctors could do that had any lasting impact. Bed rest, physical therapy and aspirin — that's all we had at Mass General. We would think nothing of giving patients as many as 20 aspirins a day, enough to cause ringing of the ears. Surprisingly, I don't remember any gastrointestinal complications from all that aspirin. Of course, when I tell my GI colleagues that today, they are horrified. The only other therapy around was intramuscular injection of gold salts. But before I got there, Walter stopped using them because one of his patients died from a cerebral hemorrhage caused by an injection of gold salts.

Even though rheumatology was a new field and medical science was not particularly sophisticated, Walter firmly believed in the importance of laboratory research. Also, he very intentionally made sure his physicians and scientists worked side by side. This was an emerging concept in the 1940s.

Walter wasn't a laboratory man himself. He spent a lot of time raising money to keep the operation running. This was decades before any substantial funding for arthritis research was available from the federal government.

The day-to-day laboratory research was done by two physician-scientists who were with him permanently — Marian Ropes and Charles Short — and by a series of research fellows who came and went over the years. While treating patients all day, I regularly interacted with Marian and Charles and the others working in the lab: the Robert W. Lovett Memorial Laboratories for the Study of Crippling Diseases. It was one of only a handful of places conducting basic research in rheumatology.

I did not get involved in any of Walter's laboratory studies. But I did some clinical research on a condition called Reiter's syndrome that turned out to be significant. The onset of this disease is usually inflammation of the urethra in men and of the cervix in women, followed by painful swelling in the joints, inflammation of the eye and, sometimes, skin disease. I wrote a paper, co-authored by Walter, about seven patients with Reiter's syndrome at Mass General. It was the first publication about Reiter's syndrome in U.S. medical literature.

Dr. Hans Reiter — for whom the syndrome was named because he published a paper on it in 1916—became a Nazi war criminal. A member of the SS, he was found guilty at Nuremberg for the deaths of hundreds of Jews at Buchenwald who were subjected to typhus inoculation experiments he designed. When this came to light in the late 1970s, I joined some other physicians in a long campaign to abandon the term "Reiter's syndrome" and replace it with "reactive arthritis." This finally happened just a few years ago.

When our paper on Reiter's syndrome was published in 1942, I was in the U.S. Army, my fellowship with Walter Bauer cut short by America's entry into World War II. I'll never forget the day— Sunday, December 7, 1941, 20 degrees below zero in Boston. Jean and I were driving to a friend's home when the radio music was interrupted to announce that Pearl Harbor had been bombed by the Japanese. Like most young men, I decided to join the Army and go off to serve my country.

Eph at 1 or 2, with his parents.

Eph with his maternal grandparents, Bessie and George Rosenberg (seated), his mother, Tillie Rosenberg Engleman (back left), and his aunt, Rose Rosenberg Daniels (back right).

Eph's grandparents, Bessie and George Rosenberg, date unknown.

Eph with his parents, about 1923.

Parents, Tillie and
Morris Engleman,
Catalina Island, 1925.

Eph's grandmother, Bessie
Rosenberg, with his aunt,
Rose Rosenberg Daniels,
Santa Cruz, 1925.

Eph holding his brother, Maurice, March 1929.

Eph in Santa Cruz, 1925.

Eph's grandparents, Bessie and George Rosenberg, in their later years.

Eph, far left, in the Fox California Theatre orchestra, about 1929.

Eph as music director of the Fox California Theatre orchestra, about 1931.

Tillie Engleman at the Golden
Gate International Exposition,
1940, and Eph, far right.

Eph, when he was a resident at Mt. Zion
Hospital, 1939.

UCSF residents and assistant residents, about 1940.
Eph: second row, far right.

Eph at his Stanford University
graduation, 1933.

Eph with his brother, Maurice, 16 years his
junior, 1934.

Engleman family, Santa Cruz, 1934. From left: Maurice, Morris, Tillie, and Eph.

Eph and his brother, Maurice, Santa Cruz, 1935.

Eph, 21 years old.

Marian Walter Sinton,
Eph's mother-in-law.

Jean Sinton, about the time she met Eph.

Jean and Eph on their wedding day, March 2, 1941.

Jean Sinton Engleman,
about 1942.

Eph during his
military service.

Eph (right) with Walter Bauer.

Dr. Engleman at the podium of the International League Against Rheumatism conference, over which he presided in 1977, with U.S. Senator Alan Cranston, UCSF Chancellor Frank Sooy, and others seated.

Section 2: Going Strong

13. The battle of Palm Springs

I walked into an Army recruiting station in Boston three months after Pearl Harbor, and I enlisted. The sense of patriotism was very strong. The United States had been attacked. There was a lot of anger at the Japanese. Everybody was talking about volunteering for military service. Times were so different then. The only thing comparable in modern times was the heightened patriotism after 9/11, but that was short-lived and, in terms of intensity, nothing compared with World War II.

During my physical exam, the doctor noted my low back pain and restriction of motion—a problem triggered by the one time I played a sport, volleyball, while a resident at UCSF. I was disqualified from serving overseas. I have to admit, I was delighted by this news.

I was assigned to the Army Medical Corps, a noncombat branch for physician-commissioned officers, and sent to Hammer Field in Fresno in the heart of the San Joaquin Valley, 190 miles southeast of San Francisco. During training, they put a disassembled gun in front of me and told me to put it back together. I had never touched a gun, and it was soon obvious I had no idea what the hell to do with it. They gave up on me and put me to work in the Army Air Forces' hospital there, where I treated service men with general medical conditions, not war injuries. It was pretty much like working in any hospital except I wore my uniform under my white coat. I wore my uniform everywhere, never civilian clothes. One night while standing in line at the movies, a little boy looked up at me and said to his mother, "Look, there's General MacArthur."

We had a commanding officer by the name of Heine — a lovely man who never seemed to be quite "with it." He recommended my promotion to captain after I was there only two or three months — a complete surprise and, I have to say, unearned. But it wasn't just me: he quickly and enthusiastically promoted everyone under his command. Before long, the Army figured out he was a bit cuckoo, and he was relieved of his duties and disappeared.

Jean was with me in Fresno, and she loved living there. We rented a little house in the Fig Garden neighborhood on the northern edge of town. The house was charming, set on a big lot and nestled in an old fig orchard. I could tell Jean was happier than she had been in Boston. For one thing, she could get warm. After enduring Boston's long, brutal winter, she welcomed Fresno's hot, dry summer and moderate winter temperatures. Also, she really enjoyed living in a small city, and Fresno had only about 60,000 residents then. She went back to school at Fresno State College and got all As earning her B.A. in Greek and Roman mythology.

After about a year, I was transferred to Palm Springs, California to be chief of a 50-bed rheumatic fever center that had just opened at Torney General Hospital, a military facility. Getting that cushy gig was entirely due to the influence of Walter Bauer, who during the war was a consultant to the surgeon general. We were good friends by this time, and I got to see him on the three or four occasions he made official visits to Torney.

Torney was unlike any hospital I've ever seen. Its six-story, pink Byzantine lookout tower appeared in the windy desert like a mirage. Before the war, Torney had been the legendary El Mirador Hotel — an old-style, luxury resort that opened in 1929 and was a favorite getaway for Hollywood royalty and other celebrities craving seclusion, dry heat, sunny weather, outstanding accommodations, and out-of-this world food.

Charlie Chaplin, Albert Einstein, and Salvador Dali were among the guests who swam in El Mirador's Olympic-size swimming pool, which had five diving boards, an observation deck, and a giant underwater window through which photographers snapped pictures. Outrageous events were a specialty of the hotel, dreamed up for publicity. One year at Christmas El Mirador featured Santa Claus at the bottom of the pool sitting on a throne beside a gaudy tree and breathing through a very long tube. Guests swam down to him for presents.

The Army bought El Mirador in 1942 and converted it into a 1,600-bed general hospital for military personnel. Like the other branches of service, the Army was taken by surprise when an epidemic of rheumatic fever felled thousands of servicemen, both overseas and on bases at home, because rheumatic fever was primarily a childhood disease, rarely seen in adults. Though it is seldom encountered in developed countries today, it can be serious, and even fatal, when it involves the heart. Joint pain and swelling are the common symptoms of this disease, which is triggered by streptococcal sore throats and spreads easily under group living conditions, especially where personal hygiene tends to be neglected, as in an army barracks.

At Torney, I had a unique opportunity to observe rheumatic fever in adults, and I wrote several papers on it. I was in charge of diagnosis and treatment, and we had about 50 rheumatic disease patients at any given time. Many had been infected months earlier and, thanks to recently introduced antibiotics, had improved considerably. They were, essentially, convalescing with us. Others still had problems, and our biggest concern was potentially fatal cardiac involvement. We never lost a patient, though.

Near the hospital were two Army Air Forces airfields that played a critical, behind-the-scenes logistical role in helping win the war, training pilots to fly thousands of urgently needed bombers and other combat aircraft from U.S. factories to overseas bases, primarily in the Pacific theater.

One Sunday night in 1945, Jack Benny broadcast his hugely popular radio show live from Torney General Hospital. His guest star was William Powell, whose silent movies I had accompanied in the late 1920s from the orchestra pit of the Fox California Theater. Benny's radio show was a big production: regular cast members Mary Livingston, Rochester, and Don Wilson performed, and there was a big orchestra. It was an outstanding show, and we gave thunderous applause to every skit, especially those with insider jokes about the nurses at Torney and the high cost of living in Palm Springs. Jack Benny did a lot to boost military morale on the home front and overseas, but for some reason his contributions have been largely forgotten, overshadowed by those of Bob Hope.

In Palm Springs, Jean and I settled into a happy domestic life together. We enjoyed doing simple things like driving to the commissary for groceries — a necessity since there were no convenient food stores. By chance, Hans Smetana — the Columbia pathology professor with whom I played Beethoven and Mozart sonatas — was also stationed at Torney, and we got into the same weekly musical routine as we had in New York.

I realized this blissful interlude was going to end when one night Jean told me she had missed her menstrual cycle. I was the one who put it into words: she was pregnant. We had been trying to conceive for some time.

Phillip was born July 19, 1944, in Torney General Hospital. Although there were no problems, Jean and our son stayed in the hospital ten days after the delivery. Three months later, Jean was pregnant again — this came as a complete surprise to both of us — and our second boy, Edgar, was born at Torney in July 1945.

When the war ended, I was transferred to Van Nuys, California, where I was chief of medicine at a military hospital for six months. I was discharged from the Army, a lieutenant colonel, at the Presidio in San Francisco.

Just prior to leaving Palm Springs, I was invited to join a respected, well-established medical practice in Los Angeles. I thought about it seriously because I would have been walking into a thriving business and could skip what I expected to be the daunting challenge of building a private practice from the ground up. But I declined, deciding it was important to settle near family in the Bay Area. And I knew that our parents would want to see a lot of their grandsons.

14. Home

For almost a year after my discharge, Jean and I and our boys lived not just close to our family but with Jean's parents in Hillsborough because we couldn't find a suitable house in our price range. Edgar and Marian Sinton couldn't have been more welcoming. Edgar tended to be a bit formal and reserved — he was the only one to wear a suit and tie to dinner. But Marian was sweet, just lovely, very nice to us.

Jean's sister Ruth, her husband, Paul Steiner, and their son Peter also lived in the Sinton house then, as did Jean's 20-year-old sister Marian, and her French governess, whom we called Mademoiselle. Like me, Paul had recently been discharged from the military. So there were 11 of us living there, plus the servants. But the house was so large and had so many bedrooms that it never felt crowded.

I liked living there. Their Danish cook Sophie always prepared excellent meals — good American food — and I got rather used to having someone wait on us at the table.

I opened my private practice in San Mateo in 1947. I was the first, and for many years, the only trained rheumatologist in Northern California. Word got out and patients flocked to me from all over the region. I worked until five or six PM every weekday and sometimes on Saturday mornings. For the first time, I was earning a nice income.

I usually made it home for dinner.

It was during this time that I started at UCSF. I paid a visit to Dr. William J. Kerr, who had recommended me to the Pratt Hospital in Boston for a medical residency seven years earlier. Still Chairman of the UCSF Department of Medicine, Dr. Kerr was delighted I turned out to be a rheumatologist because he had been the first president of the American Rheumatism Association in 1937. That a cardiologist — even one with special expertise in rheumatic fever — presided over the nation's association of rheumatologists indicates the scarcity of trained rheumatologists at that time.

Dr. Kerr introduced me to Dr. Stacy Mettier, a hematologist who ran the UCSF Arthritis Clinic. Soon thereafter, they invited me to take over leadership of that clinic. I eagerly accepted and moved my private practice to the UCSF campus on Parnassus Avenue.

Jean was pregnant when we found a house in San Mateo that we loved. We left the Sinton house with mixed feelings. It was lovely being there, but it was nice to be on our own. We moved just prior to Jean entering Mills Hospital where she delivered our beautiful daughter, Jill. Like our boys, Jill was born in July. My father-in-law, Edgar, suggested that Jean and I vacation separately during the month of October each year.

We've been in the house on Sycamore Avenue ever since. It's a handsome pre-1906-earthquake home, the oldest in San Mateo Park.

15. Revolution in rheumatology

A short amateur movie shown at an international congress hosted by the American Rheumatism Association in New York in 1949 transformed the treatment of arthritis worldwide and forever changed the field of rheumatology, for better and for worse.

I was in the ballroom of the Waldorf Astoria when Dr. Philip Hench, the highly respected chief of rheumatology at the Mayo Clinic, showed his film of a woman crippled with severe rheumatoid arthritis who tried, and failed, to rise from a chair. Twenty-four hours after an injection of cortisone, we saw her easily rising and moving around the room. Cortisone was a new wonder drug with powerful anti-inflammatory effects. We gave Dr. Hench a standing ovation. Walter Bauer and other leaders rushed to the podium, congratulating Dr. Hench for this momentous breakthrough. I don't remember with certainty if they used the word "cure," but that was the implication.

Everybody in the field immediately and wholeheartedly embraced the use of cortisone. Overnight we went from having very limited options — aspirin, gold salts, physical therapy, and hospitaliza-tion— to this. At UCSF, we were the first in Northern California to offer cortisone treatments.

Within months, however, the terrible side effects of prescribing ridiculously large doses of cortisone became apparent: diabetes, hypertension, moonface. The bubble had burst. Word quickly got out among rheumatologists through publications and meetings, and everybody modified their practice. Further complicating the situation, the patients' pain and stiffness returned when cortisone was stopped. We continued to prescribe cortisone, but in smaller doses. We still prescribe it today, now it's called prednisone.

Phil Hench shared the 1950 Nobel Prize in Medicine or Physiology for his work on cortisone. He was a very sensitive man, and he experienced severe depression because he had so enthusiastically promoted it. I have heard that his depression indirectly led to his death in 1965 of diabetes, that he apparently neglected taking insulin.

Walter Bauer could have been the guy in the spotlight for this so-called revolution in rheumatology instead of Phil Hench. He had received a big batch of a drug called ACTH—which stimulates the adrenal gland to make cortisone—from Armour Pharmaceutical Company. But instead of using it as an experimental treatment on patients, he put it in his refrigerator and forgot about it. Walter Bauer was by nature conservative in his approach to treatment.

Since the introduction of cortisone in the middle of the twentieth century, there have been two other major treatment advances in rheumatology. Methotrexate came on the scene in the 1980s, and the so-called biologics arrived in the 1990s. Joint replacements are equally important.

16. Goodbyes

My father Morris died in 1953 at age 68. He had a heart attack in Los Angeles, where my parents had gone on a short vacation. A few years earlier he had sold his pawn shop/haberdashery business and retired. Although he was under the care of a cardiologist, he was quite active, and his death was unexpected.

Looking back, I feel awful that I didn't go to L.A. to help my mother, who arranged for my father's body to be shipped home for burial. She was rather stoic about his death. When we were leaving the cemetery, she said, "Well, your father's gone and that's the way it is." No tears. She was the same way some years later when it fell to me to tell her that her beloved younger sister Rose had died tragically from an allergic reaction to a drug given during a routine medical procedure, despite Rose having alerted the doctors to her allergy. I think my mother said, "That's terrible." But that was it. I was amazed how she took each loss in stride.

The year my father died, Jean and I bought a small, three-bedroom house in the Santa Cruz Mountains on two and a half acres of land. Because I loved the Santa Cruz beach so much, I wanted a place on the ocean. But we couldn't find anything right on the beach. We put in a swimming pool and for years we went almost every weekend the weather was decent. Jean stayed there with the children a couple of summers, and I'd go on the weekends — like my father had done when I was a boy. We frequently invited people up for barbecues — family members, musician friends, people from the university — and I became quite the barbecue cook.

My mother came to live with us in either 1958 or 1959 for about a year. I don't remember exactly how this came about, but I'm pretty sure she had sold the family house on South 13th Street in San Jose. I was a little concerned my mother would disrupt our family life. But she turned out to be a wonderful guest and grandmother to our kids, who were between 11 and 15 years old then. It made all the difference in the world that Jean welcomed her so warmly.

All three of our children were bright and did well in school. All took music lessons, too: Phil on piano, Eddie on violin and Jill on cello. Like my mother had done with me, Jean coached them with their music lessons, even though she had almost no musical training. My mother was very impressed by this. I attended the children's recitals as often as possible. At one of them Phil played piano and I played violin, some excerpts from a Beethoven sonata.

Jean was a great mother. In retrospect, I don't think I was a very good father. I loved my children, but I don't think I really took care of them. Jean did. I wish I had played ball with them, sat down and done homework with them, spent more time with them.

When my mother left our home, she moved into a retirement community nearby. She died at 73 years of age in 1961 of cancer, a recurrence of the disease that had required a mastectomy in the late 1930s.

Some months before she died, I had become president-elect of the American Rheumatism Association (ARA), meaning I would be president the following year. She wasn't the type to say it, but I knew she was very proud of me.

In the late 1950s I started volunteering on various professional committees and editorial boards related to rheumatology. Although I was not an outstanding scholar, my visibility grew quickly. I was a protégé of Walter Bauer, and that carried a lot of weight. It also helped that I'm an extrovert who loves to talk and meet new people. Once, when there was an ARA meeting in San Francisco before I became president, I hosted a party for 50 or 60 people at Jean's parents' home. I remember Phil Hench and Walter Bauer being there. It was very festive with lots of delicious food and drink and music. I played the piano and sang.

My work with the ARA required a lot of travel to meet with committee members, government agencies, and the like. Once I had to leave Jean when she was in the hospital for a hysterectomy. I hated to do it. The ARA was a smaller professional society then — nothing like today's American College of Rheumatology — a large, complex organization that is truly a national force in medicine. As president, I encouraged more vigorous efforts to teach medical students and residents about rheumatology in order to improve patient care; to increase arthritis research, of which there was very little; and to generate private philanthropic support for various endeavors. All these things came about eventually, and I hope my efforts made a difference.

Walter Bauer died the year my term ended as head of the ARA.
I visited him a few weeks before his death at Mass General — the
hospital where he had introduced me to rheumatology two decades
earlier and where he had risen to become chairman of the department of medicine. Because of severe emphysema, he was in an
oxygen tent. Walter had always been a chain smoker. He looked
pretty bad. He had aged a lot and lost weight. He got out of his
oxygen tent for a smoke and so we could talk better. It was an
emotional last visit for me.

Walter continues to be remembered at an annual lecture at
Massachusetts General Hospital named in his honor, which I
helped establish and fund many years ago.

17. The transformation of UCSF

In 1964, a young man from Harvard named Lloyd Hollingsworth Smith Jr. came to UCSF as chairman of the department of medicine with a mandate to shake things up. He did. He was the driving force behind the transformation of what his Harvard colleagues— surprised by the rising star's career move — characterized as an "undistinguished" academic medical center into the international medical research institution it is today.

This transformation took many years and required Dr. Smith to wage a monumental political battle to throw out the entrenched forces, who were fiercely fighting for their jobs, their empires, and the status quo. Heads rolled, to be sure.

By then, I was both chief of the Arthritis Clinic and head of the Rheumatic Disease Group, as well as the recent president of the ARA. Still, I was bit apprehensive when Dr. Smith scheduled our first meeting, so I made a mental note of my strong points: I was a big shot on the national stage in rheumatology, I had started the West's first basic science research program in rheumatology at UCSF in 1957, and I helped launch the UCSF Rheumatology Fellowship Program—where physicians train in the sub-specialty of rheumatology — in 1958. I had also published a fair number of papers, but were there enough of them and were they up to his standards?

Perhaps my biggest advantage was that Dr. Smith and I were both protégés of Walter Bauer. Some 20 years after my time at Mass General, Walter executed a daring and brilliant strategy — one resisted by the old guard — by appointing bright young faculty members with little experience to be the chiefs of various specialty units. Dr. Smith had been Walter's chief of endocrinology.

The meeting went well enough. We reminisced a little bit about Walter and talked about what I was doing in the clinic. Nothing dramatic. Over the subsequent years I became good friends, then best friends, with the man everybody calls "Holly" Smith. He is currently associate dean emeritus of the UCSF School of Medicine. Our close friendship continues to this day.

As UCSF's stature grew, a number of important opportunities came my way, and Holly always helped me advance my career. When after a national competition, the Congress decided that the Rosalind Russell Medical Research Center for Arthritis would be at UCSF, it was Holly who said that I would be its director, and I was 66 years old then. During an National Institutes of Health (NIH) site visit, I remember so well somebody on the NIH committee saying, "Holly, don't you think that Eph is getting a little old to be the head of this thing?" and Holly said no and defended me, and that's why I'm still the director 34 years later.

18. Fiddles

I suspect that the first violin that I used, a child's violin, came from my father's pawn shop. When I was a little older and acquired an adult-size instrument, that fiddle also came from my dad's shop. I played it when I was with the orchestra and throughout medical school, the military years, and the first ten years I was in private practice. I finally realized that I was playing a pretty lousy fiddle, and it was time to get something better.

In 1957 I acquired a fine violin—one made in the early seventeenth century by Nicoló Amati who preceded and inspired future violin makers, including Antonio Stradivari and Giuseppe Guarneri del Gesù. Less than a decade later I traded it plus cash for my first Stradivari, called the Muntz, an important instrument because it is believed to be his last. Inside there is this inscription in his hand: *D'Anni 92* (92 years old). You can see he must have had a tremor from how he carved the purfling. It was in exceptional condition and its tonal quality was excellent.

I was very excited to have a Stradivari, but as time went by and I grew more sophisticated about tone, it was apparent it wasn't perfect for me, and eventually I sold it.

When I had been in medical school in New York in the 1930s, I visited the shop run by violin dealer Rembert Wurlitzer, a cousin of the Wurlitzer of organ fame. Through Mr. Wurlitzer I purchased my second Stradivari, the Jupiter (also known as the Imperator), a gorgeous violin with distinctive sap markings running vertically through its flanks. It was for many years in use at the Juilliard School, where students, including Itzhak Perlman, practiced on it.

About 15 years later, another Stradivari in exceptionally superior condition came on the market. Most violins are named for the artists who played them, but this one didn't have a name. It had been in one family for over 150 years and was rarely played. I sold the Jupiter and acquired it.

Soon thereafter, the preeminent authenticator of violins, Charles Beare of London, contacted me. To commemorate the 250th anniversary of Stradivari's death, Mr. Beare was organizing a major retrospective in Cremona — bringing home some of Stradivari's most important instruments from all over the world. He said, "If you permit me to include your Strad, we'll have to call it something, so we'll call it the Engleman Stradivari." I said that's fine with me. And so that violin became known as the Engleman Stradivari.

Jean and I arrived in Cremona a few days before the opening, and I personally delivered the violin to Mr. Beare. The Muntz and the Jupiter were also on exhibit. It was a delight to see them displayed in the gallery of the Palazzo Comunale.

After the exhibit, the Nippon Music Foundation of Japan approached me to buy the Engleman Strad, and I sold it. It is currently on loan from the Nippon Foundation to Lisa Batiashvili, an accomplished young Georgian violinist.

Selling it to the Nippon Foundation left me without a Strad, but I was not without a great violin. I owned two, in fact. In 1966 I had purchased my first violin made by Guiseppe Guarneri del Gesù — the Joachim. It was named after Joseph Joachim, the preeminent nineteenth-century violinist who once owned it. Guarneri's violins often show rough, even eccentric, workmanship and are characterized by their remarkably dark tone. Guarneri made violins for working musicians and after he died at age 46, impoverished, his instruments were largely underappreciated until Paganini popularized them. Today many eminent soloists prefer the Guarneri del Gesù.

The Joachim Guarneri is the finest violin I've ever owned, one of the most visually stunning ever created, with deeply carved edges and an almost unbelievably thick ruby-red varnish, which contributes to its depth of tone. This instrument was considered to be so important that the world authority at Wurlitzer — an Italian named Simone Fernando Sacconi, who had never traveled west of New York — personally delivered it to me, accompanied by Mrs. Wurlitzer. That's how much he thought of it. We had a little party here when it arrived, during which Mr. Sacconi begged me never to sell it because he wanted to ensure the Joachim would remain in the hands of someone who treasured it. I've kept my promise.

I also owned another Guarneri del Gesù, the Carrodus, which, according to Mr. Beare, is one of the four or five finest violins still played. It had been owned by Ossy Renardy, a young violinist who was killed in a car crash. The violin, which he had in the car with him, was undamaged.

The Joachim violin made by Giuseppe Guarneri del Gesù in 1737.

The Joachim, viewed from the back.

In 1994 the Metropolitan Museum of Art sponsored an exhibit of Guarneri violins on the 250th anniversary of his death. I still owned both the Joachim and the Carrodus, and they were displayed together in the same glass case with a sign that read, "On loan from Dr. Ephraim P. Engleman." There was a big write-up in the *New York Times*.

Not long after the party to celebrate the arrival of the Joachim, I got a phone call from Mrs. Wurlitzer, and she said to me, in effect, a young kid named Itzhak Perlman is coming to San Francisco. He's a very fine violinist and he's going to play for the first time with the San Francisco Symphony. He doesn't know anybody there. For heaven's sakes, call him, greet him, and make him feel welcome. Which I did, and that was the first time I met Itzhak. I had planned to see him again, since he was going to be in San Francisco for three or four days, maybe even take him to dinner, but he was such a sensation in his first concert that he was completely booked. So I didn't see him again at that time.

I have seen Itzhak from time to time over the years, and we stay in touch. Many years ago he called me because he was interested in purchasing one of the Strads I owned, maybe the Jupiter. Having no intention of selling it, I quoted a pretty high price, and he said, "Well, thank you very much." Obviously, it was more than he could afford then.

When we get together, we always talk about violins, yet there's another essential ingredient in performance: the bow. The finest violins were made in Italy; the finest bows were made in France, with one exception — the bows of Nikolai Kittel, often referred to as the Russian Tourte. The greatest French bows were those of François Xavier Tourte and Dominique Peccatte (early nineteenth century). In 2008 there was an exhibit in London of 50 Tourte bows organized by the bow expert and dealer Paul Childs. The Engleman I Tourte was recognized by Charles Beare as the finest of the exhibit. There's also an Engleman II Tourte. I must confess I enjoy seeing the name Engleman associated with these works of art.

Over the years I have collected excellent examples of the above bow makers. It's a small collection, but awfully good.

I also have three violins now: the Joachim Guarneri, another Stradivari — named the Engleman II Strad by Charles Beare when I bought it from him — and a copy of the Guarneri that I had made by the celebrated Luis Bellini of New York some years ago. I mention the copy because when I travel — I don't travel much now, but when I do — I always take the copy, keeping the others in a bank vault.

I've come a long way from the violin of my childhood. I play the Engleman II Stradivari in rotation with the Joachim Guarneri and its copy at my Monday evening chamber music group, at shows and recitals at my men's club, and on other occasions. Unfortunately, I have practically no sense of touch in my right hand — not from age but from unsuccessful carpel tunnel surgery a few years ago. In my left hand, a tendon of a finger slips sometimes while I'm playing. That's another major handicap. My musical friends tolerate my playing, and I still get great pleasure from it.

19. Rosalind Russell and the National Commission

The year was 1975, and there I was, pushing Rosalind Russell in a wheelchair through the halls of the U.S. Senate to lobby for public policy to help people with arthritis. I had just been elected chairman of the National Commission on Arthritis, charged by Congress to study in depth the clinical, social, and economic effects of arthritis on American society and to recommend specific actions to improve the situation. Rosalind, working closely with the Arthritis Foundation, had gotten the ball rolling in Washington, influencing powerful senators and congressmen to introduce the legislation that led to the national commission I chaired.

Like everyone who met her, I was a bit star-struck. She was not only a big movie star, but a big Broadway star. I liked her immediately. She was smart, articulate, gracious, charming and genuine. At 68, her great beauty had diminished—not only from age, but from cortisone.

When Rosalind Russell was diagnosed with severe rheumatoid arthritis in 1969, she made a courageous decision: she went public. It pretty much ended her career because studio owners and directors stopped hiring her, concerned she wouldn't be in top form.

She testified before Senate and House committees on the profound lack of knowledge about arthritis. She told them that treatment options were terrible and that research should produce break-throughs, as was the case in cancer and heart disease. It is not an overstatement to say Rosalind Russell changed the course of rheumatology and helped millions of patients.

I had been appointed to the commission because California Senator Alan Cranston —who had heard about my work in the field of rheumatology on a national level— was a chief proponent of the legislation Rosalind lobbied to have enacted. I was honored to serve. But I never expected to lead.

At our initial meeting in Bethesda, Maryland, we were sitting around the table when one of the NIH employees said, "Your first order of business is to select your chairman." A friend of mine, Dr. Howard Polley of the Mayo Clinic, stood up and said, "I nominate Dr. Engleman." This was a complete surprise, and there was no other nomination made, so I became the chairman. I accepted with mixed feelings because I knew it would be a tremendous burden in terms of the impact on my family, my wife, my private practice, and my work at UCSF.

It turned out to be an even bigger job than I expected. I was told we had to have meetings at least once a month in Bethesda and that there would be 12 public hearings in states scattered across the country. My attendance was required at all of them. My job was to direct the commission, coordinate its 18 members' work in subcommittees, and deliver a National Arthritis Plan to the U.S. Congress. We had one year.

Rosalind Russell and Eph working together at a meeting of the National Commission on Arthritis, 1975 or 1976.

Rosalind Russell (right) with other commission members.

Rosalind Russell in *Auntie Mame,* 1958, with Jan Handzlik as Patrick Dennis.

Rosalind Russell

One enormous task was to assess current activities rela
patient care, medical education, and research. What we learned
was shocking: 55 percent of arthritis patients were receiving no
medical care at all; 21 states had fewer than five rheumatologists,
and six of those states had none; of 114 medical schools, 26 had no
full-time rheumatologist. Two-thirds of medical schools reported
to us that their educational programs in rheumatology were inad-
equate. The National Institutes of Health was devoting only 1.5
percent of its research budget for a disease that afflicted more than
10 percent of the population.

A second major undertaking was to solicit input at public hearings.
We heard from more than 300 witnesses — mostly patients, ranging
in age from under 10 to over 90, many of whom were in wheelchairs and on crutches — in Tucson, Houston, Boston, Seattle, and
eight other cities. Their heartbreaking stories revealed a huge and
hidden population experiencing often-intolerable pain, disability,
economic decline, poor medical care, family crises, depression, and
unrelenting anxiety. I've never forgotten one woman who summed
up her life like this: "The most profound thing anyone ever told me
about rheumatoid arthritis is that it wouldn't kill me, but it sure
would make me wish I was dead."

They asked the same questions over and over: Why doesn't the
government mount a full-scale attack on arthritis? Why is it so
difficult to find doctors trained to treat arthritis? Why aren't there
better treatments? Why doesn't somebody educate patients about
what they can do to help themselves?

We delivered a multi-volume National Arthritis Plan to Congress, but I can sum up the situation we investigated in four words: it's a big mess!

Within a couple years, the federal government acted on many of our important recommendations. The one I'm proudest of is creation of the National Institute of Arthritis, Musculoskeletal and Skin Diseases. (I never found out who slipped "skin diseases" in there.) Also significant, the NIH established a large network of multipurpose arthritis centers. These thrived for decades, but many closed in recent years due to severe budget cuts. (The one at UCSF is doing quite well, I'm pleased to say.) NIH funding for arthritis research doubled or tripled, depending on the time frame over which you measure. (Regrettably, over the past decade the NIH has done an about-face and dramatically reduced funding for arthritis research.) Rheumatology was added to the curriculum at all medical schools.

The last meeting of the commission was in San Francisco, and Rosalind attended. I hosted a dinner party at my home and transported everyone there by bus. Rosalind was in great spirits. She sang songs from *Gypsy* and *Wonderful Town* as I accompanied her on the piano. She didn't use her wheelchair that night. She was feeling no pain — quite literally, because earlier in the day she asked me to prescribe opiates. Only several weeks later I heard on the TV news that she died at her home in Beverly Hills of cancer.

20. A very long way

Rosalind Russell died in November 1976, and within six or eight months the United States Congress decided to honor her by creating an arthritis center in her name. It would receive a one-time grant for arthritis research in the neighborhood of $800,000. They turned the selection process to find a suitable site over to the National Institutes of Health.

I spearheaded the UCSF team that wrote an application and found out we were among the finalists. Rosalind's husband, Broadway producer Freddy Brisson, wanted it to go to UCLA, presumably to be closer to her friends in the film industry. Several NIH representatives made a one-day site visit to UCSF, and I took them to San Francisco General Hospital, where we wanted to construct an immunology research laboratory for Dr. Ira Goldstein, an internationally recognized expert on inflammation in rheumatologic diseases. That was the focus of our pitch.

We were selected as the site and in 1979 held a ceremony in the lobby of San Francisco General to mark the opening of the Rosalind Russell Medical Research Center for Arthritis. Freddy, Rosalind's husband, was emphatic that we include the phrase "medical research center" in the name despite the fact that it's a mouthful. Although I wasn't crazy about it at the time, I'm forever grateful to him. He and his son, Lance Brisson, were in attendance, as were Mayor Dianne Feinstein, UCSF Chancellor Frank Sooy, UCSF

School of Medicine Dean Julius R. Krevans, and a couple of people from the NIH.

We received a lot of newspaper publicity and, consequently, within a week two women who were good friends of Rosalind came to me. I didn't know them. Betty Folger Miller (later Betty Cooper) and Leita McBean volunteered the idea to have some laypeople help raise money for the Center. The conversation impressed me very favorably and I encouraged them to go ahead. We set about creating a board of directors. Betty was our first chairperson, and for many years, board meetings were held at her spectacular home on California Street atop Nob Hill.

The Rosalind Russell Medical Research Center for Arthritis became the fundraising arm for the UCSF Division of Rheumatology. Over the years, we've raised in excess of $50 million from private individuals, and that money has made the critical difference between UCSF having an extremely good rheumatology research program and having one of the top two or three in the world.

At first, all the research was basic science — laboratory investigations on the causes and mechanisms of arthritis. The field has opened up through stunning advances. The center played a role — often a leadership role — in UCSF research that contributed to six new arthritis drugs approved by the Food and Drug Administration. We provided substantial funding to launch and sustain a major arthritis clinical trials center. An investigative team supported in part by the center has identified dozens of genes associated with rheumatoid arthritis and lupus—making them potential targets for new therapies. We funded, and continue to fund, clinical research on reducing heart disease in rheumatoid arthritis patients, understanding and screening for depression in arthritis patients, and preventing the shortened lifespan and serious medical problems among many adults whose lupus started in childhood. Recently, we helped launch a major, ongoing effort to reduce the health disparities between the haves and the have-nots afflicted with arthritis. And over the years the Rosalind Russell Medical Research Center for Arthritis has provided financial help to well over a hundred physicians during their three years' training in the UCSF Rheumatology Fellowship Program, where they became not only sub-specialists in rheumatology but leading scientists and practitioners in the field.

As it did from the beginning, the center continues to support basic research with impressive results. One team has defined a number of key molecular processes that take place when people's immune cells mistakenly attack their body's own tissue and cells, which triggers autoimmune arthritis, including rheumatoid arthritis and lupus. They've also identified important therapeutic targets for experimental drugs. Other teams of UCSF basic scientists are making discoveries that are almost certain to lead to valuable clinical tests. As a result of their work (and that of their colleagues elsewhere), we expect to soon have a test to monitor bone erosion without waiting for x-rays; another test to predict, at the time of diagnosis, whether a rheumatoid arthritis patient will have a mild or severe course of disease, which helps the doctor decide whether to be aggressive in treatment; and yet another test that predicts which patients will do well (or poorly) on specific drugs or combination therapies.

Directing the Rosalind Russell Medical Research Center for Arthritis has been the most gratifying part of my career. I'm still the director and I very much enjoy the fundraising I do on behalf of the center. I am proud of its success and also of the financial contributions and commitments Jean and I have made to it. We've come a very long way from when clinic waiting rooms were cluttered with wheelchairs and patients were hospitalized for weeks and given huge doses of aspirins. When I started working with Walter Bauer, I never imagined such progress in my lifetime, and I certainly never imagined that I would have anything do to with it.

21. The Family

I was an intern at Mt. Zion Hospital in 1937 when I was invited to join The Family club. As well as being a venue for making lifelong friends, The Family club has allowed me to indulge my passion for being on stage. Seventy-six years after joining — and nearly 90 shows and concerts later — I'm still at it.

In 1901, William Randolph Hearst published a poem in his newspapers by Ambrose Bierce that seemed to predict President William McKinley's death by an assassin's bullet. McKinley was assassinated a little later, and Hearst was so caught up in the firestorm over the poem that it ended his hopes of running for president. When the Bohemian Club banned from its premises the *Examiner,* a Hearst paper, 14 members who were editors and reporters at the paper — led by Pop Hamilton — quit the club, formed a new one, and called it The Family. The Family is pretty much a copy of the Bohemian Club — a private men's club devoted to the arts — only much smaller.

In 1989 I wrote the music, lyrics, and the narrative to a show (we call it a *row*, rhymes with *cow*), about this history. It's called *Keep Young*, which is the club's motto. Here are the lyrics of a duet sung by the characters Ambrose Bierce and William Randolph Hearst:

Our Tradition

We're Ambrose Bierce and Willie Hearst
Selling papers must come first
We always emphasize the worst
That is our tradition.

We said McKinley was a pain
He had big business on the brain
We even blamed him for the Maine
Accused him of sedition.

To stretch McKinley on his bier
A picture that we all hold dear
Amusingly, this is the year
We'll send him to perdition.

Willie likes your slashing wit
It's obvious you've scored a hit
We'll tone it down a little bit
For the next edition.

We're Ambrose Bierce and Willie Hearst
Selling papers must come first
We always emphasize the worst
That is our tradition.

The show ends in a scene in which Pop Hamilton escorts President McKinley on a heaven-sent visit to The Family. It was such a big hit that we revived it twice.

During a typical show I stand before the audience, tell the story, and set up the songs for the Songbirds (that's our glee club) and the Ever Faithful (our orchestra). We've done concert versions of Broadway shows, including *Guys and Dolls* and *My Fair Lady,* as well as programs of music by popular composers like George Gershwin and Irving Berlin. We always get a standing ovation, and the enthusiasm is especially high on Wednesday nights when wives are in the audience. On Tuesdays it's men only.

Once a year there is a weekend at our Portola Valley Family Farm called the *flight.* The stork is our emblem, and it refers to the flight of the stork. We always perform a flight noon concert. I played violin with the Ever Faithful for more than 70 years. We have done quite a bit of classical music and a lot of Broadway. At almost every performance, I found an excuse to play a violin solo. I stopped playing with the orchestra more than 10 years ago because I always give the spoken word, and I can't do both.

My biggest success on stage at The Family was as Mick Jagger in 2006 — I was 95 years old at the time. I wore a wig, flamboyant sunglasses, a black leather vest, and the classic Rolling Stones red-tongue T-shirt and sang, "I can't get no satisfaction. I try and I try and I try." That was in one of our variety shows. I've also impersonated Jack Benny in conversation with Jascha Heifetz, and played Maurice Ravel when he met George Gershwin for the first time. Gershwin wants to take music lessons from Ravel. Ravel asks him what he does and how much he gets paid, and after hearing the answer, says, "Maybe I should take lessons from you."

We have many talented men at The Family, and everything usually goes very well on the production side. At one of the shows, however, someone put a microphone on me an hour before curtain which mistakenly was not turned off. I was on a floor above where the audience was gathering, and everything I said and did was heard, including going to the bathroom. When I came onstage, I got a lot of applause.

Because of my theatrical contributions, on one side of an outdoor stage at the Farm there's a plaque on a redwood tree that reads "Dedicated to Ephraim P. Engleman." On the other side is an old plaque dedicated to Pop Hamilton. So it's quite an honor.

By a huge margin, I am the oldest member of The Family club, not only in terms of my age, but for the length of time I've been a member. I've been there 23 years longer than anyone else in the club. There are two classes of membership: associates, like me, are the ones who perform or work backstage on sound, lights, and so forth. Then there are the resident members, who are essentially the audience, who may do other things if they wish but are not obligated. In the case of the associates, work is required because they don't pay an initiation fee, and their dues are halved. When I joined, there were no dues for associates. By the time they started charging us half the full rate, I was emeritus because I'd been there 25 years, and the emeriti don't pay dues.

So I have never paid dues. Maybe because I felt a little guilty, I thought of a way to contribute. I created the Family Fund about 20 years ago to help creative prospective members to join who cannot pay the dues, as well as members who've fallen on hard times and can't continue to pay them.

Right now I'm writing my script as MC for our concert version of *Kiss Me Kate*, coming up next month. (I write everything out long-hand. I've never touched a keyboard). We rehearse once a week for a couple of months. When we have a show such as *Kiss Me Kate* or *South Pacific* we have the problem of casting the female roles. Obviously we have no females in our club. I am very much opposed to drag. So what we do is maybe put on a lady's hat, or it might be a shawl, but that's it. The role is done just as a man would do it, in a man's voice, and not in falsetto.

Each member is called a *child,* and the president of the club is the *father.* During the skit at The Family's 99th birthday party, the MC called out the name of a child who is a terrific actor and put the guy in the chamber on the left. Then he added a child who is a professional musician to that chamber, then a gifted singer, then a really good writer. Then he said some magic words to mix them all up and make "the perfect child," and who stepped out of the other chamber? Me.

22. The Other Family

Jean and I have three kids. Kids? At 66 to 69 years of age, they're hardly kids.

Our oldest, Philip, played in piano recitals, was valedictorian of his San Mateo High School class, Phi Beta Kappa at Stanford University, M.B.A., Stanford Business School, and received his M.D. in the charter class at the UC San Diego School of Medicine. He published the first report of the lung disease called pulmonary hydralizing granuloma, which is a benign disease often mistaken for metastatic lung cancer. He was chief of pathology at Kaiser Hospital in San Jose for 30 years, and now, alas, he is retired.

Next in line is Edgar. He was student body president at San Mateo High School, a graduate of Harvard College magna cum laude, concertmaster of the Harvard orchestra, and a Rhodes Scholar finalist. Like me, he received his MD from the Columbia University College of Physicians and Surgeons. He is professor of pathology and medicine at Stanford University, and founder and director of the Stanford Blood Center. He developed and implemented the first blood test to prevent transmission of the HIV virus via blood transfusion. He is also principal inventor of the first FDA-approved immunotherapeutic drug for treatment of cancer of the prostate (known as Provenge) and is author or co-author of more than 275 medical papers.

And then there's our youngest, Jill. As a child she quit her cello lessons when, contrary to promises, she was asked to perform in a cello recital. She graduated from UC Berkeley and was an elementary school teacher at a public school for four years. She married a great guy, who became the fourth of what are now five physicians in our family, including a granddaughter. (As an aside, I will mention that we finally acquired a lawyer in the family, a grandson who is a deputy attorney general of California.)

Jean and I have six grandchildren and two great grandchildren.

23. Goodies

The longer you live, the more goodies you receive.

One of the goodies I'm most proud of is the Ephraim P. Engleman Distinguished Professorship in Rheumatology at UCSF. I like knowing there will always be an "Engleman Professor" there. (In fact there will be two: last year UCSF established the Jean S. Engleman Distinguished Professorship in Rheumatology.)

UCSF also awarded me its most prestigious award, the Medal of Honor. I've received Gold Medals from both the American College of Rheumatology "in recognition of major contributions" to the field and the Columbia University College of Physicians and Surgeons. The Columbia medal is kind of ironic considering I was such a poor medical student, but they honored me for "excellence in clinical medicine." Also, I'm an honorary member of the rheumatology associations of six countries, including China. I led three medical delegations there in the 1980s as president of the International League Against Rheumatism and helped the Chinese rheumatologists persuade their government bureaucracy to permit organization of the Chinese Rheumatism Association.

I never really thought about my age until three or four years ago when people starting calling it to my attention. The Columbia medical school magazine ran a profile that opened with this para-

graph: "Think of George Burns minus the cigar. At 98 and count-
ing, Ephraim P. Engleman '37, the dean of American rheumatology,
cautions against overexercising and early retirement." When I
turned 100, there were stories about me on the *NBC Nightly News*
and CBS television and an article in the San Francisco *Chronicle*.
California Governor Jerry Brown issued a proclamation, calling me
"a model of longevity and strong work ethic." *Stanford Magazine*
ran a feature a few months ago entitled "The Last of a Class."
Apparently, no one else who graduated in 1933 is still around,
much less working. Public radio did a little piece earlier this year,
too, making much of the fact that I still see patients. And earlier
this month the *Huffington Post* published an interview on the
occasion of my 102nd birthday, calling me "a shining example of
longevity" and saying, "It's hard for us to not be amazed by Dr.
Engleman's graceful aging."

A *Washington Post* writer, working on a story last year about
how to ensure older doctors are competent to treat patients, asked
me to comment and quoted what I've told everyone at UCSF: "By
all means, let me know if I'm slipping — and I'll get the hell out
of here." When the reporter mentioned that Stanford and other
hospitals require periodic physical and cognitive exams of their
physicians over 75, I wish I had said, "All physicians should be
tested once in a while regardless of their age."

Everybody wants to know why I've lived so long. It's fortunate that
for the past 97 years I've been participating in research that helps
to answer that question: Lewis Terman's study on genius — which

I joined when I was five — and subsequent work by UC Riverside psychologists Howard S. Friedman and Leslie R. Martin. They spent 20 years drawing upon the vast quantities of detailed information in Terman's archives to determine the characteristics most strongly associated with longevity.

Friedman and Martin are the first whose findings come from following a single set of participants from childhood to death. In their 2011 book, *The Longevity Project,* they identified four major predictors of long life, and I seem to have all of them.

The best childhood personality predictor of longevity, I was a bit surprised to read, is conscientiousness. It's so un-sexy. But it does describe me both as a child and an adult. As long as I can remember, I have been prudent, persistent, well-organized, and dependable. I'm oversimplifying here, but Friedman and Martin speculate that conscientious people live longer because they probably don't smoke or drink too much, follow their doctors' orders and, consequently, are generally healthier than others. They also speculate that conscientious people might have certain biological distinctions — perhaps something to do with levels of chemicals, like serotonin, in the brain.

The best social predictor of a long life, they write, is "a strong social network." I had to ask what that means. It's the term social scientists use to describe being active and engaged with other people. That's me, for sure. No surprise about that one.

For a man, a happy marriage is also very important. (Not so much for women, who apparently often live long lives despite not-so-happy marriages.) I have the supreme pleasure of being in love with and devoted to my wife of 72 years, Jean. We have always enjoyed spending time together, and we still do. My children were happy to learn that a couple's mutual compatibility is a strong factor in predicting their children's longevity.

The fourth major predictor is having good, challenging work. I love my work, and at 102, I go to my office three days a week, where I see patients and run the center. I keep my supremely patient and highly reliable secretary, Marie Ducousso, busy full time because I work from home quite a bit on my days off. I still attend medical conferences and symposia on campus and see colleagues in the Bay Area, old and new, to keep up with clinical and research advances.

I know I am *by far* the oldest practicing rheumatologist, and I'm just one year shy of the world record for oldest practicing physician held by Leila Denmark, who was 103 when she retired. She lived to be 114.

I have no intention to stop any time soon.

24. Ten tips on longevity

1. Be sure to select parents with the right genes.

2. Choose the right spouse. Encourage sex — with your wife, that is. Children are optional.

3. Enjoy your work, whatever it is, or don't do it. Under no circumstances should you retire voluntarily.

4. Exercise is overrated. Exercise only if you must.

5. Avoid vitamins, organic foods, fish oil, and other so-called nutrients. Don't bother with special diets. Just don't weigh yourself.

6. Keep your mind active. Have many interests, such as music, reading, writing, crossword puzzles, and poker.

7. Avoid travel by air. Travel by car instead. It's much more exciting.

8. Don't fall. When in doubt, use a cane. You'll be amazed how much respect you get when you use a cane.

9. Avoid heart attacks, stroke, cancer, arthritis. When it's convenient, see a doctor, especially a rheumatologist.

10. Be happy and lucky. But most important, keep breathing. This is absolutely critical to longevity.

Eph and Jean at a party, 1940s.

Tillie Engleman holding Philip (left)
and Edgar Engleman, August 1946.

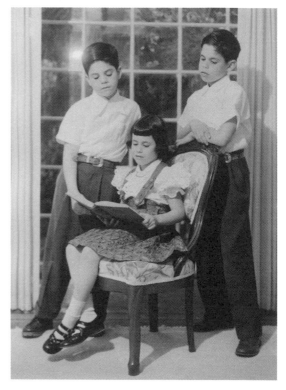

From left: Edgar, Jill, and Philip Engleman.

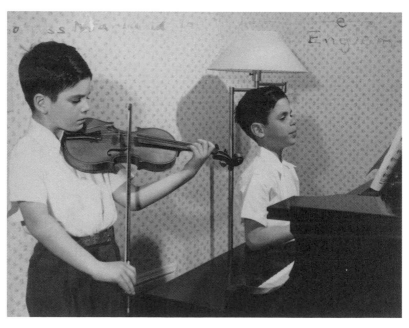

Edgar (left) and Philip Engleman.

Edgar and Jill Engleman, about 1951.

Philip, Jill, and Edgar.

Eph's father, Morris, 1952.

Morris with Jill on her horse, Rosie Red, about 1953.

Eph in 1967
©Gabriel Moulin Studios

Eph and Jean, 1984.

From left to right: Eph, Betty Ford, and Rosalind Russell, 1974.
Official Photograph, The White House.

Rosalind Russell's husband, Freddy Brisson, and San Francisco mayor, Dianne Feinstein at the dedication of the Rosalind Russell Medical Research Center for Arthritis, 1979.

Lloyd Hollingsworth (Holly) Smith Jr., about 1964.

Leita McBean

Betty Folger Miller

Eph at the Family Farm, 1972.

Eph receiving his Family club award of appreciation, 1969, flanked by Chris Trowbridge (left) as Sir Appreciation and club father, Otto Pfleuger (right).

Eph, about 1980.

Eph at the Family Farm, 1980.

Eph as Mick Jagger in a skit at The Family club, 2006.
Photo courtesy of Michael Mustacchi.

Eph at a party. Photo courtesy of Michael Mustacchi.

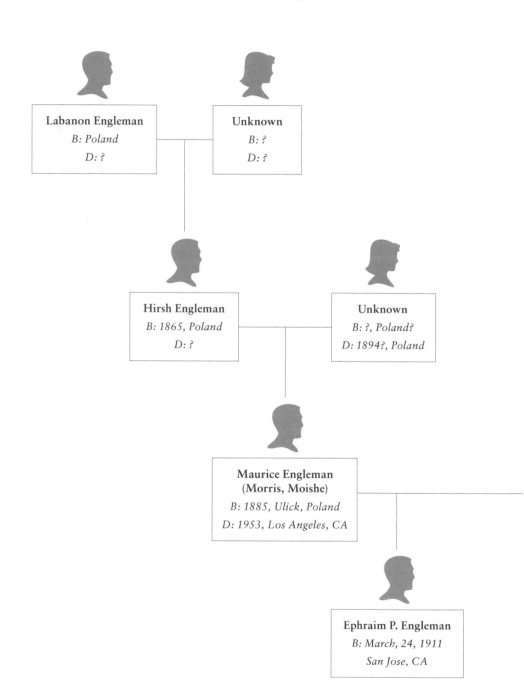

Labanon Engleman
B: Poland
D: ?

Unknown
B: ?
D: ?

Hirsh Engleman
B: 1865, Poland
D: ?

Unknown
B: ?, Poland?
D: 1894?, Poland

Maurice Engleman
(Morris, Moishe)
B: 1885, Ulick, Poland
D: 1953, Los Angeles, CA

Ephraim P. Engleman
B: March, 24, 1911
San Jose, CA

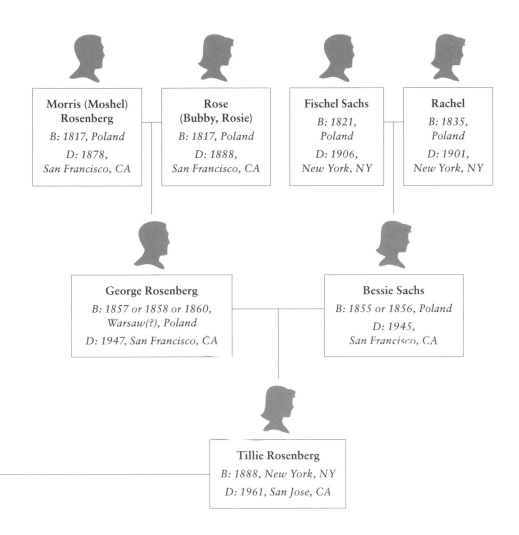

Four generations of Englemans. Research for this book produced some surprises. Five of Eph's eight great grandparents were identified for the first time. Public records list three different dates of birth for George Rosenberg and two for Bessie Sachs Rosenberg.

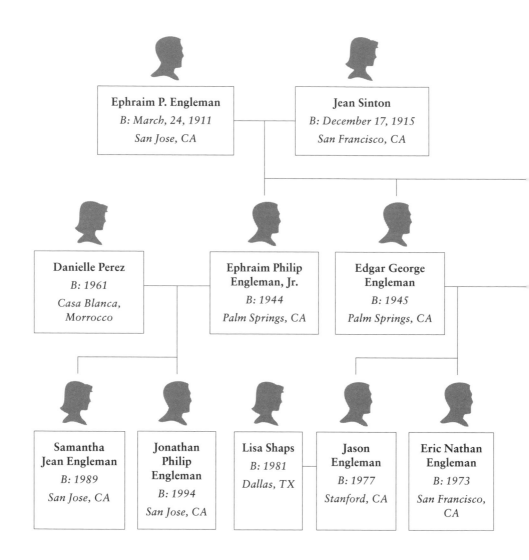

Ephraim P. Engleman
B: March, 24, 1911
San Jose, CA

Jean Sinton
B: December 17, 1915
San Francisco, CA

Danielle Perez
B: 1961
Casa Blanca,
Morrocco

Ephraim Philip
Engleman, Jr.
B: 1944
Palm Springs, CA

Edgar George
Engleman
B: 1945
Palm Springs, CA

Samantha
Jean Engleman
B: 1989
San Jose, CA

Jonathan
Philip
Engleman
B: 1994
San Jose, CA

Lisa Shaps
B: 1981
Dallas, TX

Jason
Engleman
B: 1977
Stanford, CA

Eric Nathan
Engleman
B: 1973
San Francisco,
CA

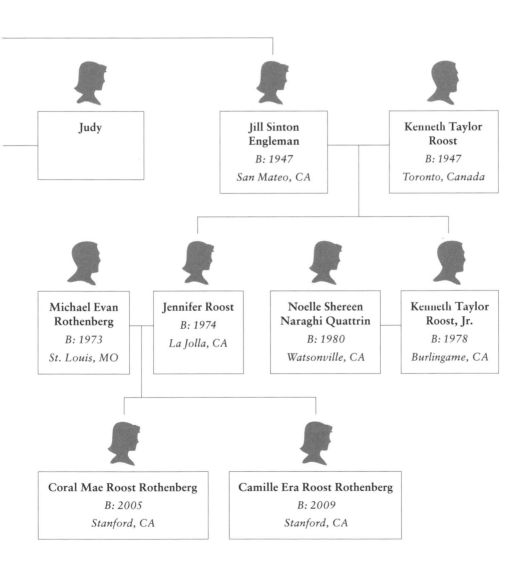

NOTES

"EPE" is used throughout this section to designate Ephraim P. Engleman.

Chapter 2. "Early years"

On EPE's ancestry: EPE's earliest traceable ancestors are his great-grandparents on his mother's side—Tillie Rosenberg's grandparents—Morris (Moshel) and Rose (Bubby, Rosie) Rosenberg. They were both born in 1817 in Poland. Her maiden name is unknown. They had nine children; George, Tillie's father, was the eighth and, according to one source, was born in Warsaw. Morris died in San Francisco in 1878. Rose died there a decade later.

EPE's other pair of maternal grandparents—Bessie Sachs Rosenberg's parents—were Fischel and Rachel Sachs. He was born in 1821 in Wola Uhruska, a Polish town 129 miles southeast of Warsaw. (The Nazis set up the Sobibór extermination camp near there in 1942, and an estimated 200,000 Jews died in its gas chambers.) Rachel was born in Poland in 1835. Her maiden name could not be found. Fischel and Rachel married in 1854. Bessie, the second of their three daughters, was born in either July 1855 or January 1856. Fischel and Rachel emigrated to New York in 1882. (Some evidence suggests that Bessie may have emigrated three or seven years earlier.) Rachel died in New York in 1901. Fischel died there on February 19, 1906.

Bessie Sachs and George Rosenberg—both Yiddish-speaking, Polish Jewish immigrants—met in New York and married there in 1880. Family lore has it that their marriage was arranged by a matchmaker and they did not see each other until their wedding day. George sold cigarettes on the streets of the Lower East Side and he was naturalized in New York in 1884.

Little is known about EPE's paternal ancestors. His grandfather, Hirsh Engleman — who emigrated to the United States from Poland ahead of his family — was born in 1865 and died in Berkeley, California. Hirsh's father's name was Labanon Engleman, and he was born in Poland.

A family myth. During interviews, both EPE and his brother Maurice said that their grandparents George and Bessie Rosenberg lived to be more than 100 years old and died within weeks or months of each other. In fact, Bessie died when she was 89 or 90 and George died two years later somewhere between 87 and 90 years of age. George's exact date of birth is uncertain. Three dates of birth appeared in various public records: May 5, 1857; April 1858; and March 1860.

Chapter 7. "My father, Morris"

On Morris Engleman and the Yiddish Art Theater. Although Morris Engleman told his family he had been a child actor with the Yiddish Art Theater in New York, this was not the renowned troupe with the formal title, Yiddish Art Theater. That company was formed in 1918 by Maurice Schwartz 20 years or more after Maurice moved to California. Michael Stoller, director of Collections and Research Services in New York University's Division of Libraries, writes,

> There was a generic term, "Yiddish art theater," which denoted a movement led by young, relatively un-Americanized immigrants with radical political views and close connections to the cultural world, who sought to elevate the quality of Yiddish theater... [Morris Engleman] was... perhaps making an anachronistic reference, looking back from a later era, when the concept of the Yiddish "art theater" was well established in the Jewish community. [He] may simply have thought of [himself] as having been associated with

this relatively sophisticated, culturally aware branch of Yiddish theater, in contrast to the more common, unsophisticated theater that had predominated up to the early years of the 20th century.

Chapter 9. "Stanford years"

On the Stanford Gaieties. In the 1932 Stanford Yearbook, *The Quad,* the following article mentioning EPE appeared under the headline "The Big Game Gaieties." It was accompanied by a photo of a chorus line of eight women in what look like maids' uniforms, and the caption "Eight Little Co-Eds Standing in a Row."

> Someone is bound to be cheated in a half-page review of such an all campus affair as the Big Game Gaieties; yet it is safe to say that those who were fortunate enough to get seats were thoroughly compensated, and more, for their efforts. The innovations in staging by Harold Helvenston were a distinct novelty though hardly adequate to set off the many spot numbers. The music and rhythm were potentially very good, and on occasion the orchestra blared forth with foot-tapping choruses. The girls looked quite capable of "stepping high, wide, and handsome" had they been given more than one real opportunity. Eph Engleman, with a Fanchon and Marco background, kept the show rolling merrily along between numbers and shared honors with Lloyd Phillips, Jacqueline DeWit, and Virginia Elston in clever bits of dialogue and stepping.

Chapter 10. "Columbia: Anything goes"

On anti-Semitism in American medical schools in the 1930s. A *New York Times* article (May 14, 2012) describes the widespread practice of enforcing quotas for Jewish medical students in the 1930s. It specifically cites the Columbia College of Physicians and Surgeons, which EPE attended during this period: "The proportion of Jews in the student body fell to less than 5 percent in 1938 from nearly half in 1920." The subject of the article is an exhibition called *Trail of the Magic Bullet: The Jewish Encounter with Modern Medicine, 1860 – 1960,* focusing on the emergence of European and American Jews as innovators in medicine "despite their status as outsiders frequently scorned by the medical establishment."

Chapter 11. "Jean: Dancin' to Anson"

<u>On Jean Sinton Engleman's parents and ancestors.</u> Edgar Sinton, born in 1889, was an attorney — a graduate of Hastings — with a small private practice on Montgomery Street in San Francisco. His family wealth originated with his grandfather, Simon Koshland, a Bavarian immigrant who started a very successful San Francisco–based whole-sale business in 1879 buying wool from around the world and selling it in Boston to New England's booming textile mills.

Jean's mother, Marian Walter, was born in 1894, the third of three children (the first girl) of Isaac N. Walter and Caroline Greenebaum. She attended Miss Muirisson's school for girls. She didn't graduate from high school because her parents took her out of school to take the baths at Baden-Baden, then enrolled her in a Parisian boarding school. Jean's grandfather, Isaac Walter, had immigrated from Germany in his teens and settled in San Francisco, where in 1858 he and five brothers started a wholesale and retail business selling carpets and furnishings. It was called D. N. & E. Walter & Co., and it still exists. Their timing couldn't have been better: The population of San Francisco quadrupled in the subsequent 40 years and almost everyone needed new furniture after 1906 earthquake.

On the Sinton home in Hillsborough: When Jean Sinton Engleman's family lived there, the address was 325 Ranelagh Road. Today it's 120 Roblar Avenue. When Robert A. Swanson, co-founder and CEO (and later chairman) of Genentech Inc., lived there, he did a major renovation, switching the front entrance to what, in Jean's time, had been the back of the house on the Roblar Avenue side of the property.

Chapter 16. "Goodbyes"

On EPE volunteer service in the field of rheumatology:

Elected, Appointed, and Invited Positions: National

- Consultant in Rheumatic Diseases to Veterans Administration in Western States Area, 1950–1960

- Member, Graduate Training Program Committee, National Institute of Arthritis and Metabolic Diseases, 1957–1961

- Member, Editorial Board, Arthritis and Rheumatism, 1957–1961

- Chairman, American Rheumatism Association (subsequently the American College of Rheumatology) Committee on Relationship with Arthritis and Rheumatism Foundation, 1960–1965

- First Vice-President and President-Elect, American Rheumatism Association, 1961–1962

- Member, National Board of Directors and its Executive Committee, Arthritis and Rheumatism Foundation, 1962–1963

- Member, Medical and Science Committee and its Executive Committee, Arthritis and Rheumatism Foundation, 1962–1963

- Member, Council of National Institutes of Arthritis and Metabolic Diseases, 1962–1963

- President, American Rheumatism Association, 1962 – 1963
- Member, Steering Committee for the Surgeon General's Conference on Prevention of Disability from Arthritis, Airlie House, Warrenton, Virginia, May 5 – 8, 1965
- Chairman, Public Education Committee, Arthritis Foundation, 1965 – 1968
- Chairman, Government Health Program Committee, Arthritis Foundation, 1966 – 1968
- Visiting Lecturer, Mayo Clinic, May 10 – 12, 1967
- Visiting Lecturer on Medicine, Harvard University, November 1 – 30, 1967
- Visiting Physician-in-Chief, Visiting Professor of Medicine, Robert B. Brigham Hospital, November, 1967
- President, National Society of Clinical Rheumatologists, 1967 – 1969
- Member, Editorial Board, Postgraduate Medicine, 1971 – 1976
- Member, Medical Advisory Committee, The American Lupus Society, 1974 – 1981
- Chairman, National Commission on Arthritis and Related Musculoskeletal Diseases, 1975 – 1976
- Member, National Arthritis Advisory Board to the National Institutes of Health, 1977 – 1981

Elected, Appointed, and Invited Positions: State and Local

- Consultant in Rheumatic Diseases to San Francisco Veterans Administration Hospital, 1950 – 1970

- Chairman, Medical and Scientific Committee, Northern California Chapter of the Arthritis Foundation, 1954–1956

- President, Northern California Rheumatism Association, 1958–1959

- Consultant in Medicine and Rheumatic Diseases to U.S. Army Letterman General Hospital, San Francisco, 1960–1976

- Chairman, Medical Advisory Committee, The National Foundation, San Francisco Chapter, 1962–1963

- Chairman, California State Governor's Conference on the Prevention of Disability in Arthritis, Los Angeles, California, May 19–21, 1967

- Chairman, Arthritis Program Directors, California Regional Medical Program 1974–1976

- Member, Commission on Systemic Lupus Erythematosus Research, California State Department of Health, 1976–1984

- Chairman, Government Affairs Committee, Northern California Chapter, Arthritis Foundation 1980–1982

- Chairman, Board of Directors, Northern California Branch of Arthritis Foundation, 1982–1984

- Chairman, California State Council for Government Affairs, Arthritis Foundation, 1982–1986

- Member, California State Arthritis Council 1986–1988

Elected, Appointed, and Invited Positions: International

- Secretary for the Americas, International League Against Rheumatism, 1957–1961; 1965–1966

- Member, Board of Consultants, *Archives of Inter-American Rheumatology,* 1957–1966

- Member, Advisory Committee on Arthritis, International Society for Rehabilitation of the Disabled, New York, 1963–1967

- Member, World Health Organization, Expert Advisory Panel on Chronic Degenerative Diseases, 1963–1984

- President, XIV Congress of the International League Against Rheumatism, San Francisco, June 26–July l, 1977

- President-Elect, International League Against Rheumatism, 1977–1981

- President, International League Against Rheumatism, 1981–1985

- Chairman, World Health Organization–International League Against Rheumatism Task Force on Arthritis, 1982–1984

- Member, Editorial Board, *Japanese Journal of Rheumatology,* 1986

On EPE service in elected positions at UCSF:

- President (and cofounder), Association of Clinical Faculty, University of California, San Francisco, 1970–1971

- President of Executive Medical Board of University of California Hospitals and Clinics, San Francisco, 1973–1974

On EPE and Jean S. Engleman philanthropy:

- Established the Jean S. and Ephraim P. Engleman Endowment for Rheumatology Research at UCSF, 1996

- Established the Ephraim P. Engleman Resident Research Preceptorship at the Rheumatology Research Foundation at the American College of Rheumatology, 2005

- Established the Dr. Ephraim P. Engleman '37 Scholarship at the Columbia University College of Physicians & Surgeons for a medical student with an interest in music, 2010

On EPE service on nonmedical boards:

- Director, Crescent Porter Hale Foundation, supporting Bay Area community, education, and arts programs, 1950 –
- Chairman, Family Foundation, providing financial assistance to members of The Family club in need and their widows, 1998 –

On EPE's friendship with Walter Bauer. Around 1950, EPE wrote words for a parody of Cole Porter's "You're the Top" to honor Walter Bauer and sang the song at a party for him in Boston. Here is the first stanza.

"You're the Top" for Walter Bauer

You're The Top, Dr. Walter Bauer;
You even top the Empire Tower.
You're the best by climate test, We're gaspin'.
Yes, you ride the crest even on bed rest; here's to Aspirin!
You're the top, you're the strength in muscle;
To eat your dust, Henchmen* have to hustle.
M.G.H.** is the coolest joint of the lot.
But if gold salts are the bottom, you're The Top.

* "Henchmen" refers to Dr. Philip Hench.

** "M.G.H." refers to Massachusetts General Hospital

Chapter 17. "The transformation of UCSF"

On Lloyd H. Smith's decision to come to UCSF. In a 2007 biography of Lloyd H. Smith Jr., MD, his 1947 Harvard School of Medicine class-mate Marvin Sleisenger — appointed by Dr. Smith as chief of medicine at the San Francisco VA Medical Center in 1967 — identifies four reasons Holly Smith decided to come to UCSF to chair the Department of Medicine: 1) The basic sciences had just moved back to the UCSF campus from UC Berkeley, where they had been transferred after the 1906 earthquake. 2) NIH support of biomedical research was growing exponentially. 3) In 1959, the Stanford University School of Medicine moved from San Francisco to Palo Alto "allowing control of San Francisco's major teaching hospitals to be unified." 4) The dawn of jet travel meant UCSF faculty members — no longer remote and isolated — could participate in professional meetings anywhere.

Chapter 18. "Fiddles"

On making a copy of the Joachim Guarneri. Simone Fernando Sacconi was an international authority on violins made in Cremona, Italy, and author of the seminal book *The Secrets of Stradavari*. Mr. Sacconi thought that the Joachim was one of the finest Guarneri violins he'd ever seen, so much so that he wanted to make a copy of it. When EPE was on a trip to Europe, he left the violin with him. But Sacconi died before making the copy, and it was created instead by his protégé Luis Bellini.

Chapter 20. "Rosalind Russell and the National Commission"

On EPE's leadership of the National Commission. Commission member Milton Silverman, PhD, included the following letter in a special commemorative book presented to EPE. Dr. Silverman was both head

science writer for the San Francisco *Chronicle* and on the faculty of the
UCSF School of Medicine Health Policy Program.

> To Eph Engleman –
> Slavedriver!
> Dictator!
> Tyrant!
> Interrupter of sleep!
> Telephone addict!
> Maniac!
> Already you're so mean, in twenty-four hours I could make
> you a city editor . . .
> But it was good to have been aboard. It's not a bad product.

On *The Arthritis Book*: In 1984, EPE and Dr. Silverman coauthored
The Arthritis Book: A Guide to Patients and Their Families.

Chapter 22. "The Family"

On lyrics. A song from the musical, "Keep Young," written by EPE
about The Family club:

"The Family Hymn"
From the gloomy desert of our earthly lives
Our fellowship will lead us where joy ever thrives;
Poor is our beginning but our purpose is high.
Whatever fortune deals us, our hope will never die.
Here's to our Family, may it grow and prosper
Always keeping music and love as our gospel.
We pour the libation on our beloved hearth
We dedicate our Family to laughter, music and art.
To our Family — God give us joy!

Chapter 23. "Goodies"

On EPE honors:

- Public Tribute, Arthritis Foundation and American Rheumatism Association, June 8, 1973

- Honorary Member, Uruguay Rheumatism Society, 1963–

- Honorary Member, Rheumatism Society of Spain, 1970–

- Honorary Member, Japan Rheumatism Association, 1973–

- Award for Distinguished Contributions to the Clinical Programs of the Hospitals and Clinics and School of Medicine of UCSF, June 3, 1982

- Honorary Member, Australian Rheumatism Association, 1985–

- Honorary Chairman, Inaugural Meeting of Chinese Rheumatism Association, Nanning, China, April 20–21, 1985

- Honorary Member, Société Française de Rhumatologie, 1981–

- Honorary Member, The Gold-Headed Cane Society Inc., University of California, San Francisco, 1986–

- Master of American College of Rheumatology. The first such award for members of the ACR "who have set the highest professional standards in advancing the art and science of rheumatology," 1987–

- Honorary Member, The Chinese Medical Association 1987–

- Honorary Member, International League Against Rheumatism, 1989–

- Endowment of Ephraim P. Engleman Distinguished Professorship in Rheumatology, UCSF, established, 1991

- The Medal of Honor, UCSF. "The UCSF Medal is the most prestigious award given by UCSF to individuals who have made outstanding personal contributions in areas associated with the University's health science mission and whose efforts mirror the goals and values of UC San Francisco," 1999

- Presidential Gold Medal, American College of Rheumatology. "The highest award that the ACR can bestow, awarded in recognition of major contributions to Rheumatology," 2002

- Gold Medal, Columbia University College of Physicians and Surgeon. "For excellence in clinical medicine," 2007

- Master of Pan American Rheumatology, Pan American League of Associations for Rheumatology, 2012

Acknowledgment

This book would not have come into being without the invaluable assistance of my collaborator, Matthew Krieger, who gave structure and shape to many hours of recorded interviews. His extensive research likewise enriched the story, and I'm grateful to him.

Special thanks

Peter Biddulph

Maurice Engleman

Joe Evans, Archivist,
San Francisco Symphony

Gabriel Moulin Studios

Daniel Hartwig,
Stanford University Archivist

Polina E. Ilieva, UCSF Archivist

Stephen Kiyoi, Library Director,
Barnett Briggs Medical Library

Tom McCutchon,
Columbia University Archivist

Michael Mustacchi

Stephen E. Novak, Head
Archivist, Columbia University
Medical Center

Aldo Panattoni

Stewart Pollens

Bill W. Santin, Columbia
University Registrar's Office

Carmen Sierra, Columbia
University Medical Center Student
Administrative Services

Ruth Steiner

Michael Stoller, Director of
Collections and Research Services,
New York University's Division
of Libraries

Richard Schwarzenberger

Design

Ashton & Partners

Photo credits

Cover and title page: Kit Morris.

Photographs of the Joachim Guarneri del Gesù violin following page 82 by Stewart Pollens, courtesy of Peter Biddulph.